ADVANCE PRAISE FOR *THE SECRETS OF PICKING A COLLEGE (AND GETTING IN!)*

"The college application process can seem daunting, but this book breaks the process down into logical, manageable steps. Everyone loves a secret. These are secrets you can use, share with your best friends, and pass along to your younger brother or sister. There are over 600 tips in this book. Here's one more: Read the book. It should be your first step on the path to college."

> **—Marjorie Savage, Parent Program Director, University of Minnesota and author, *You're on Your Own (But I'm Here If You Need Me): Mentoring Your Child During the College Years***

"College advice books tend to come in several forms: some are light and breezy to read, but ultimately shallow and conventional in their thinking. Others have great insight, but it is often encased in leaden, academic prose. The authors of this book have skillfully combined the best of both worlds. This book is easy to read, clearly organized, and very specific in its advice. It is also extremely thoughtful in how it treats each step of the admission process. I plan to use it with my own students."

> **—Jon Reider, Director of College Counseling, San Francisco University High School; former Senior Admission Officer, Stanford University; and co-author of *Admission Matters: What Students and Parents Need to Know about Getting Into College***

"*The Secrets of Picking a College* takes the clutter away from the college process, breaking down the stages into bite sized chunks. The questions posed to the students throughout the book really drill down to the nuanced questions students should ask themselves as they think about where they want to spend the next four years as a student and a lifetime as an alum. Sharing with students and families an actual reader rating card that admissions officers use to evaluate each component of the application is worth its weight in gold! A valuable resource for students, parents and counselors!"

—Beth Ann Burkmar, Associate Director of College Counseling, The Hun School of Princeton, Princeton, NJ; former Regional Director of Admissions, University of Pennsylvania; and former Admissions Counselor, Drexel University

"Informative, current and logical, *The Secrets of Picking a College* is full of important information on a wide variety of topics, yet is concise and easy to understand. Individual topics are covered in a detailed and helpful manner. It will make you think about the college search process in a more thorough and wide-ranging way. I wish every family I work with would get a copy."

—Alyssa O'Brien, Director of College Guidance, Lawrence Woodmere Academy, Woodmere, NY and former Admissions Reader, Northeastern University

"If you read one book on the college process–this is the one you want. Straightforward, spot-on advice to streamline the college exploration and admission process, improve outcomes, and reduce stress for students and families. Professional insights on what really happens in the college admission world presented in a readable format students can put into practice immediately."

—Barbara T. Conner, Director of College Counseling, Foxcroft School, Middleburg, VA, and Creator of #FiveFirstChoiceColleges

"*The Secrets of Picking a College* captures the essence of the process and provides excellent tips and suggestions to students (and parents!) who are just beginning this journey. Having two sons who went through this process a few years ago, I can say that it would have been helpful to them to have a similar "Guide" handy since they were eager to try to figure it all out themselves."

—Diane Freytag, Director of Counseling and Advising, The Overlake School, Redmond, WA

"It would take hours, even weeks, to gain the knowledge on one's own that is so accessibly offered in this guide. The authors of this book did their audience a huge favor by doing a lot of the hardcore research and web searching that has taken me over a decade to acquire as a full-time college counselor. The websites offered here are particularly impressive, and the advice is sound, easy to grasp, and invaluable for any student and family searching for the right fit."

—Kelly B. Richards, Director of College Counseling, St. George's School, Providence, RI

"A guide for *all* college-bound students packed with practical pointers and compiled specifically for students. *The Secrets of Picking a College* is like having a college coach by your side. Filled with advice from college professionals – including admissions officers – this book is easily accessible and is a must-read."

—Alicia J. Linsey, Counselor, Lexington High School Lexington, MA, and founder and independent counselor, The Academic Advancement Group

"*The Secrets of Picking a College (and Getting In!)* does a *fantastic* job of capturing the 'moving target' of college admissions. Its easy-to-follow format, complete with web links for digging deeper and finding the latest updates, make it a *must-have* for high school students. It not only answers standard college related questions, but also answers important questions that students may not otherwise know that they should ask."

—Sandy Aprahamian, Independent Educational Consultant, EDNavigators LLC

"*The Secrets of Picking a College* will not be a secret for long. This virtual encyclopedia of the college admissions journey will become the 'go to' resource for parents and students alike. While this book describes every aspect and nuance of the college search (including mastering a calculator!), it presents the treasure trove of material in easy-to-read, delineated sections. *The Secrets of Picking a College* delivers the most up-to-date, practical compendium available today of the ever-evolving landscape of college admissions."

—Franca Rawitz, Independent College Counselor & Founder, ReadySetCollegeNYC

"The strategies, tips and techniques suggested in this exemplary book include information which I have gleaned through years of experience, seminars and conferences. Families who read every word, or even flip through pages and skim chapters at different times throughout the college application and transition process will find illumination on this complex, holistic process."

—Laura O'Brien Gatzionis, Educational Advisory Services, Athens, Greece

"These 600+ tips and strategies are clear, easy-to-understand and will give students insights into the often complicated college admissions process. Choosing a college list, if done correctly, can be a fun journey of self-exploration and growth. Students and their families can use this book as a resource to maximize positive outcomes and increase college acceptances."

—Jill P. Madenberg, Independent Educational Consultant and Certified High School Guidance Counselor

"Hundreds of tips with catchy headings ("Best-Kept Secret," "Reality Check," "Epic Fail!") jump off the pages, making it simple for even the busiest (or *laziest!*) teenagers to find them. Parents, too, will appreciate the ease of honing in on concise explanations, suggestions ... and warnings."

—Sally Rubenstone, Senior Advisor, College Confidential

THE SECRETS OF
PICKING A COLLEGE (AND GETTING IN!)

THE SECRETS OF
PICKING A COLLEGE (AND GETTING IN!)

OVER 600 TIPS, TECHNIQUES, AND STRATEGIES REVEALED

LYNN F. JACOBS, JEREMY S. HYMAN,
JEFFREY DURSO-FINLEY, AND JONAH T. HYMAN

Professors' Guide™
Series Book

JOSSEY-BASS™
A Wiley Brand

www.TheSecretsOfPickingACollege.com

Published by Jossey-Bass
A Wiley Brand
One Montgomery Street, Suite 1000, San Francisco, CA 94104-4594—www.josseybass.com

Jossey-Bass books and products are available through most bookstores. To contact Jossey-Bass directly call our Customer Care Department within the U.S. at 800-956-7739, outside the U.S. at 317-572-3986, or fax 317-572-4002.

Wiley publishes in a variety of print and electronic formats and by print-on-demand. Some material included with standard print versions of this book may not be included in e-books or in print-on-demand. For more information about Wiley products, visit www.wiley.com.

Library of Congress Cataloging-in-Publication Data
Jacobs, Lynn F., 1955-
  The secrets of picking a college (and getting in!) : over 600 tips, techniques, and strategies revealed / Lynn F. Jacobs, Jeremy S. Hyman, Jeffrey Durso-Finley, and Jonah T. Hyman. – First edition.
        pages cm. – (Professors' guide)
  Includes bibliographical references and index.
  ISBN 978-1-118-97463-6 (paperback), 978-1-118-97507-7 (ePDF), 978-1-118-97465-0 (epub), and 978-1-118-97464-3 (Mobi)
  1. College choice–United States–Handbooks, manuals, etc. 2. Universities and colleges–United States–Admission–Handbooks, manuals, etc. 3. Universities and colleges–United States–Entrance requirements–Handbooks, manuals, etc. I. Hyman, Jeremy S. II. Durso-Finley, Jeffrey, 1968- III. Hyman, Jonah T., 1998- IV. Title.
  LB2350.5.J38 2015
  378.1' 61–dc23
                                        2015027081

Cover design: Wiley
Cover image: Purdue University © GettyImages/E+

Printed in the United States of America

FIRST EDITION

HB Printing   10 9 8 7 6 5 4 3 2 1
PB Printing   10 9 8 7 6 5 4 3 2 1

MEET THE AUTHORS

Dr. Lynn F. Jacobs is a professor of art history at the University of Arkansas, having previously taught at Vanderbilt University, California State University Northridge, the University of Redlands, and NYU.

Jeremy S. Hyman is founder and chief architect of Professors' Guide™ content products and lecturer in philosophy at the University of Arkansas. He has also taught at UCLA, MIT, and Princeton University. Together, he and Lynn are authors of *The Secrets of College Success: Over 800 Tips, Techniques, and Strategies Revealed* (WWW .PROFESSORSGUIDE.COM)—a book you might enjoy reading once you've gotten in to the college of your choice. Lynn and Jeremy blogged for two years at *US News & World Report* (WWW.USNEWS.COM/ PROFESSORSGUIDE) and offer the "Gimme an A! The Secrets of College Success" multimedia presentation (WWW.GIMMEANA.COM) annually at many colleges.

Jeffrey Durso-Finley has been director of college counseling at the Lawrenceville School, a comprehensive, selective international boarding school in Lawrenceville, New Jersey, for the last ten years. Before that, he served for eight years as assistant director of admissions at Brown University, where his responsibilities included all aspects of recruitment, selection, and matriculation of potential students. A member of the National Association for College Admission Counseling (NACAC) and the Association of College Counselors at Independent Schools (ACCIS), and a frequent contributor to a wide range of national education publications and professional conferences, Jeffrey has helped thousands of students get in to the colleges of their choice.

Jonah T. Hyman is a beginning senior at Haas Hall Academy, a math and science charter school in Fayetteville, Arkansas. His interests include transportation engineering, maps, number theory, game shows, as well as all things patterned. Jonah scored triple-800s on the SAT (he shares his secrets in this book) and is currently in the throes of the college-picking—and, hopefully, getting-in—process.

CONTENTS

TO YOU—THE FUTURE COLLEGE STUDENT

College.

For some students it's something to look forward to: a chance to get away from home, to study something new, to make new friends, and, in the end, get that much-treasured college degree. For other students it's a source of worry: What will it be like? How will I fit in? Will I be able to do the work?

And then there's the college-application process. For virtually everybody starting the (in many cases) two-year process it seems like a lot. So many choices, so many things to do, so hard to get in, so little information about what colleges are looking for, so many ways to mess up. And, if that weren't enough, it all seems so much out of your control. How can you really know what any of the schools are like and whether you'd fit in? How can you really improve any of your standardized test scores or write an application that'll distinguish you from the thousands of other students wanting to go to that school? How will you know what to say about yourself on the personal statement or to some nameless interviewer trying to size you up? Finally, how will you ever round up enough money to pay for college at all? The thoughts swirl and pretty soon you're feeling confused and in many cases even overwhelmed by it all.

It doesn't have to be this way. Imagine there were a book that cast light on the process: that showed you all the different stages of the college-application process and told you what to do at each stage to maximize your chances of getting in to the very best colleges—the ones right for you.

This is that book—a book that covers all the major "moments" of the college-application process in a series of over 600 tips, techniques, and strategies that show you just what to do at each stage of the process. You'll first learn about the different kinds of colleges and how to locate the type that best fits your intellectual and social personality. Then, you'll learn how to use various resources to compose your initial list: general-purpose and college-specific websites, your college counselor, college nights, and visits by college reps, financial aid and scholarship tools—you'll learn how all of these can be used to your best advantage. Next, you'll find out all you need to know (and then some) about the all-important college tour: when to visit and what to do on your visit; what questions to ask on your visit and whom to ask them of; whether to attend a class, visit a dorm, or have an interview; and finally, how to evaluate and compare the colleges you've visited.

From there, it's on to the standardized tests: you know, the dreaded ACT and SAT tests—including the newly revised 2016 SAT. There'll be specific and detailed tips for each section of each of the tests—concrete things you can do before, during, and after the test to maximize your scores. Following that, we give you our best tips and strategies for putting together your applications: how best to do the personal essay on the Common App (including the newly revised 2015–2016 essay prompts); how many extracurriculars to list (and which ones colleges consider best); how to get great letters of recommendation from teachers and your counselor; how to answer those supplemental (and sometimes bizarre) questions put forth by particular schools; and, most important, how to present yourself and your achievements to best advantage. And, if that wasn't enough, there's a special piece detailing what admission officers most look for in applications.

And finally, you'll find tips for making your final choice among the (hopefully many) offers you've received for admission and aid. You'll learn things to do—and not do—in evaluating the alternatives; what to do if you've been wait-listed at a school; how to evaluate (and in some cases improve) the financial aid offer you've received; and finally, how to spot those features in the college—and in yourself—that are most likely to guarantee you a productive, and enjoyable, four or five years of college.

We've assembled a team of experts to guide you through the college application process, each of whom brings different knowledge, expertise, and experience to the book. Who better than a pair of professors to show you •what makes one college better than another •how to evaluate the requirements, curriculum, and majors at the different colleges •what to look for when visiting a class and talking to a professor or undergraduate advisor, and, most important, •how to assess the quality of the education you're going to receive at each of the colleges? And who better than a seasoned high school counselor, previously an admissions officer for ten years at a major university, to tell you •what colleges are looking for in an application •how to construct the personal statement, extracurriculars, and supplemental questions to maximize your chances of getting in •how to approach your teachers and counselor for the best possible recommendations, and •what factors to consider in making your final choice among the (hopefully) many colleges you've gotten in to? Last but not least, who better than a high school student, who's in the very midst of applying to college and who has gotten a perfect score on every standardized test he's taken, to not only •share his tips for acing the SAT and ACTs but also to •offer suggestions on managing the stress that's an inevitable part of every college search?

And if that wasn't enough, we've added tips that we've gathered by interviewing dozens of admissions officers whom we've met as we made our own college tour; and a special appendix in which a major admissions officer reveals to his colleagues (and now, to you) the criteria his university uses in admitting students (an amazing behind-the-scenes document).

We're out to change the college application process in America: to shed light on what for many students is an opaque, unpredictable, and anxiety-provoking process, and, in so doing, to level the playing field for all of those who aspire to join the 22 million students now in college. But, more than that, we hope to offer tips, techniques, and strategies that will work for *you*—that will show you the way to take ownership of the college application process and, hopefully, to get in to all the colleges of your choice.

You can do it. We will show you how.

Lynn, Jeremy, Jill & Jonah

We'd like to hear from you! If you have a question or comment—or if you'd like to contribute a tip or share an experience for the next edition of this book—e-mail us at:

- lynn@professorsguide.com

- jeremy@professorsguide.com

- jeffrey@professorsguide.com or

- jonah@professorsguide.com.

Or, if you'd like to share a tip in real-time with the over three-million students applying to college this year, post a comment at WWW.TSOPAC .COM/TIPS or tweet it @professorsguide. Maybe someone else could benefit from your insight!

Top 10 Reasons to Read This Book

10. **The tips are really good.** Written wholly by experts, the book provides high-value tips, techniques, and strategies for picking—and getting into—the colleges of your choice.

9. **The book covers all the major topics.** From first thinking about college to visiting the colleges, from taking the ACT or SAT to composing your application, from figuring out the finances to making your final choice—it's all here, with insider tips for every stage of the process.

8. **The information is quick.** Top 10 lists, Do's and Don'ts, Most-Asked FAQs, 7 Biggest Secrets, 21 Must-Ask Questions, 10-Step Plans—all the advice is bite-sized and easy-to-digest. And our *Professors' Guide* icons help you navigate your way through the book and might even provide a little entertainment along the way.

7. **The information is up-to-date.** All the new realities of the college-application procedure are covered, including the 2016 revised SAT and the revised, 2015–2016 Common App essay prompts. And we offer hundreds of URLs—many of them little-known—that will guarantee that you'll be fully informed in real time of any changes that are occurring.

6. **The tips are practical and specific.** No abstract theories here or general descriptions of the various stages of the process, just concrete, easy-to-follow tips that tell you exactly what to do—and not do—at every step along the way.

5. **The advice makes sense of the process.** The tips, techniques and strategies take what for most students is an inscrutable, perplexing, and in some cases, painful process and make it transparent, easy-to-understand, and (as much as is possible) rational.

4. **The book addresses the psychological dimensions**. We know that applying to college can be a roller coaster of emotions, so we offer you tips for minimizing anxiety, overcoming self-doubt, and, most of all, putting yourself forward in the best possible light.

3. **Each section of the book stands on its own**. Unlike some guides, you don't have to read this book cover to cover; you can pick it up and read at whatever stage of the process you're at.

2. **The information is not available elsewhere.** Trust us, we've read virtually every other book about picking a college, surfed every website we could get our hands on, and talked to dozens of admissions officers and professional counselors, and no one tells you the insider secrets we reveal in this book.

And the number one reason you should read this book:

1. **The tips will really maximize your chances of getting in.** The advice in this book has worked for thousands and thousands of students—and it will work for you!

The Professors' Guide™ Icons

 EXTRA POINTER. An additional tip that applies to a special situation.

 5-STAR TIP. A really high-value suggestion that you should be sure to use.

 BEST-KEPT SECRET. One of the things no one wants you to know but will be really helpful.

 REALITY CHECK. An invitation to step back and assess what's really going on.

 RULE OF THUMB. A general principle that will work in most (but perhaps not all) situations.

 EPIC FAIL! A giant blunder that should be avoided at all costs.

  IOHO. (IN OUR HUMBLE OPINION). Our perspective on some controversial issue. Not everyone will agree.

ON THE WEB. A useful link for getting additional tips or more information on a specific subject.

 BONUS TIP. For those who can't get enough, one more tip.

 FLASH! Late-breaking information that you'll want to know.

1 STARTING YOUR SEARCH

Starting any big project is always intimidating. And starting the college search is particularly so, since there's so much pressure associated with the process that everyone going through it—even those with the calmest possible temperaments—is going to have periods of feeling totally stressed out. The worries are many: How do I know where to apply? Will I have good enough scores on the SAT or ACT? Are my high school grades or class rank up to snuff? Do I actually have to be interviewed? What should I write on the personal essay? Will I get in where I want to go? Will I be able to afford where I want to go? Could I be making a decision that will ruin my career possibilities after college—or even ruin my life? Do I even know what career I want to have? And how does anyone actually manage to survive applying to college, anyway?

We know that, for many, this can be a tough process. But it doesn't have to be as hard as a lot of people make it. It's a lot easier if you take it step by step. And, more important, it is a lot easier if you have clear, straightforward, and simple advice about what to do at each stage of the process—not to mention if you know some of the insider secrets. That's what we're here to give you. To get you started off on the right foot—and to help you get acquainted both with the colleges and with yourself—we start off with some basics and explain:

▶ The 10 questions you should ask yourself as you begin your college search

▶ Learning the landscape: the 6 major kinds of colleges

▶ The 8 things that make better schools better

10 Questions to Ask Yourself as You Begin Your College Search

Most people start their college search by looking outward: they look at websites, talk to parents, teachers, counselors—maybe even read books! But really the best way to start is by looking inward. That's because with so many colleges, which differ in so many ways, it's really important to get in touch with *your* priorities and values before you start on the path to applying to—and picking—a college.

Going to college is a huge life change and you want the college you choose to be in line with who you are and what you want out of college. So take the time to read over, and think carefully about, these questions:

1. What reasons do you have for wanting to go to college? Although this might seem like such a no-brainer that there's no point in answering it, take some time to generate and write down all the reasons you might have for wanting to go to college. Do you want to get a world-class education? Do you want to prepare for some lucrative career? Are you looking to expand your social life and, in the best case, meet that special someone? Are you hoping to break free of your parents and develop a greater sense of independence? Do you just have no other idea of what to do with the next four or five years of your life? Whatever your reason or reasons, having a list and referring to it from time to time can help you determine more clearly what you want to get out of college and help you judge if particular colleges will really provide you with what you are looking for.

2. Do you have a single passion, or lots of broad interests? Some high school students have a particular area of study or an activity that they know is their true love and that they are absolutely certain that they want to pursue for the years to come. Been interested in climate change since you were 10? Always wanted to study bats? Been intrigued by international relations for as long as you can remember? Then you might want to think about colleges that are specifically devoted to that pursuit or have special programs in the area. However, if you like lots of subjects or just learning for the sake of learning, then a more general college, with strengths in lots of fields, might be just what you're looking for.

 REALITY CHECK. Be careful not to confuse a passion with a passing interest: there are many tales of a "passion" that faded after the first semester of college. And don't feel bad if you don't yet have a passion—most people in high school (and even beyond) don't.

3. Have you had any experiences at a college (perhaps in summer programs or concurrent enrollment programs), and what did you learn from them about what you like or don't like in a college? Some high school students have already had some experiences in a college setting, which can provide you with a leg up in sorting out what you might want to look for when choosing a college. If you're one of these students, ask yourself whether you liked the kinds of classes you took; whether you liked the living arrangements at that sort of college; whether you liked the kinds of students they had at that college; whether you liked being away from home; and so on. How you felt about a proto-college experience can provide you with important clues about what you might like in a real college experience.

4. Which courses in high school did you like and not like—and, most important, why? Reflecting on your educational experiences in high school can help you figure out what kind of educational experiences you want to have in college and what kinds you want to avoid. Did you like classes that were smaller and had lots of discussion or did you think larger classes where the teacher mainly lectured were more to your liking? Did you like classes that emphasized creative thinking or ones in which memorization was the main mode of study? Did you prefer classes that emphasized group work or ones with more individual work? Thinking about what learning experiences worked best for you can provide models for what kind of instruction you'll value in a college.

5. Do you enjoy classes that challenge you intellectually, or do you prefer easier classes? Do you like to have classmates that are as smart (or smarter) than you, or do you prefer to be at the top of the class? Naturally, no one wants to attend a school where everything is over their head or everyone is smarter than he or she is, but that shouldn't be a major worry because the college-selection process usually prevents these outcomes. However, you do have some choice about whether you want to be at a place where the students are academically gifted or study really hard—and the professors gear their courses toward smart, hard-working students—or a place where students are less academically inclined and the professors lower their expectations (and their course content and assignments) accordingly. Knowing your level of comfort—or discomfort—in challenging (and, in some cases, competitive) settings can be a help in knowing what sort of college to aim for.

6. Do you prefer to have more freedom in selecting your courses, or do you like having a predetermined curriculum? While high schools tend to have fairly strict requirements and relatively few electives, colleges vary between ones with large numbers of required courses and ones with extremely few courses you have to take (some even have an "open curriculum" in which there are no requirements). Do you like the idea of having control over much of your college program or would you rather the college structure your courses for you? Would you like fixed, set-out majors or would you like the possibility of designing your own? Knowing how you like to structure your education can help you evaluate whether the requirements at the various colleges you might be considering are right for you.

7. Do you like being in a place with lots of extracurricular activities going on—and, if so, what kinds of activities might you like to engage in? If you are a person who is always going out on the town, you're not going to be happy in a town where everyone clears out on the weekends and there's nothing to do. But that same town might be just fine for the person who just wants to hang out in the library all week long. Everyone has different kinds of interests, so consider how high a priority it is for you to attend a school with lots of social life and parties, many sporting events to watch, sports opportunities for you to participate in, a lively arts scene, an emphasis on community service or political action, a religious community that suits you, or other activities that interest you. Of course, interests can often develop or change, so consider not only what you like doing now but also what you think you might want to explore a little down the road.

8. Are you looking for a place where the student body is diverse, or would you like most of the students to be pretty much like you? Consider the level of diversity (social, political, gender, ethnic, religious) at your current school and how you experience it: Are you in a high school with mostly the same kinds of students, and would you welcome the opportunity to interact at college with different kinds of students? Or are you in a high school with great diversity and are just fine with that. Or do your high school experiences make you realize that you'd rather be with students more like yourself? Whatever your answer is, you should take it into account when thinking about colleges: with over 4,000 choices you should be able to find one with a student body you feel comfortable in.

9. What kind of town or city do you like to live in, and where would you like it to be? Do you like the idea of life in the big city or is a rural small town more to your liking? Or perhaps life in a smaller town with easy access to the big city? Is there a particular region of the country—or a particular kind of climate—that you feel is where you'd most like to be? Keep in mind you have to live in the place for four or five years—and "living" is more than just taking courses.

10. Do you want to get away from your parents or do you want to keep one foot in the nest? Distance from home is often a major factor in selecting a college, because, many students like the idea of being able to come home for holidays and weekends. On the other hand, some students want to stay as far away from the coop as they can. Know which type you are.

REALITY CHECK. Once at college, students often find that the easy drive home is actually longer than they'd like to be driving on a regular basis. And besides, the activities at college (whether academic or otherwise) end up being quite a bit more fun—or, in the case of upcoming exams and paper due dates, more pressing—than making the trek home. So try to think through the realities of the situation—how much you want to spend time with your friends vs. time you spend with your family even now.

Learning the Landscape: The 6 Major Kinds of College

Now that you've had a chance to reflect a little on your own experiences, aspirations, values, and expectations, it's time to turn to the colleges themselves—the places where you'll be spending, and enjoying, the next four, five, or six years of your life. But before beginning to consider any particular colleges—whether ones you've heard of or will hear of as you carry out your college search—it's important to understand the major differences among kinds of college and what these differences might mean to you. So here are some of the main distinctions to consider at the very outset of your college search:

1. College vs. university. Although people talk all the time about "college," actually, if you're being precise there's a real difference between a "college" and a "university." A university is an institution of higher education that offers both undergraduate and graduate degrees, while a college offers only undergraduate degrees. The name of the school is the giveaway: if the name is the *University of X* or *X State University,* it's a university, and if the name is *X College* or *X-County Community College,* it's a college.

At universities there tends to be more of an emphasis on research (though this doesn't mean that the teaching isn't great, since researchers can often incorporate their research into their teaching). And generally, universities will be larger, with larger departments, many more course offerings, and more instruction (especially in introductory courses) done by graduate students or lecturers. Colleges, on the other hand, typically emphasize teaching, so you might find smaller classes, more student-focused faculty, and, in many cases, a more supportive and less anonymous environment.

EXTRA POINTER. Many universities are made up of separate "colleges," such as the College of Arts and Sciences (which is the "Liberal Arts" College by another name), the College of Education, College of Business, College of Engineering, College of Health Sciences, and the College of Architecture. But, basically, you're still going to a university, even if you're in one of these colleges. In most cases, you can take classes in different colleges and switch between them if you want.

REALITY CHECK. Some universities have so-called Honors Colleges, which they market as equivalent to an elite, highly selective college. If you're thinking of going to one of these, take a hard look at how many classes you will take as separate honors classes and how many regular classes you will take. In our experience, even when you're in the Honors College at the University of X, you're still at the University of X—and not in the fancy, marquee college that your honors program claims to be equivalent to.

   2. Public (or state) vs. private. *Public* institutions—which include the state university system as well as community- and city colleges—are partly financed by tax dollars, whereas *private* universities and colleges are financed only by private sources of funding, such as tuition and donations. It's usually the case that for *in-state* residents, public colleges are cheaper than private colleges (though, in some states, well-capitalized private colleges can compete on price with the state university system). And although in some, especially economically depressed, states public institutions might have less good facilities than richer private schools, there's a good number of private institutions that are financially strapped and hence not as well equipped and staffed as one might think.

REALITY CHECK. Community colleges and city colleges will in almost every case be cheaper than state universities and easier to get in to.

BEST-KEPT SECRET. Some state universities, especially in larger states, try to make up for shortfalls in state revenues by charging the full, out-of-state price to students not from their home state (this can easily be three or even four times the in-state price). If money is an issue, in many cases *private* colleges will be cheaper than out-of-state public colleges. (However, if you can pay the whole bill, you might want to consider out-of-state public universities, where your ability [and willingness] to pay big bucks might increase your chances of admission.)

3. 4-Year vs. community (or 2-year) college. 4-year colleges (or universities)—which, for many students, take five or six years to complete—culminate in a *bachelor's* degree of some sort (most commonly a BA—bachelor of arts—or BS—bachelor of science—but also possibly a BFA—bachelor of fine arts—BSW—bachelor of social work—BEng.—bachelor of engineering—or BArch.—bachelor of architecture).

By contrast, community or 2-year colleges—which, for many students, especially working students, take three, four, or even more years to complete—offer a variety of *associate's* degrees (typically an AA—associate in arts—AS—associate in science—or AAS—associate in applied science). The AA and AS degrees are meant for students who plan to transfer to a state university for their last half of college and typically parallel the first two years of a bachelor's program at a 4-year college. The AAS degree is usually meant to be a vocational degree, leading to careers in such fields as health care, criminal justice, paralegal, IT management, and many others (indeed in many cases the community college partners with local industries to place graduates in jobs in their chosen field).

4. Big vs. small. Colleges come in an unusually wide variety of sizes and, especially for students whose level of comfort and enjoyment depend on the size of group they'll be interacting with, this can be a key factor to consider. *Mega* universities are those with over 50,000 students; there are only a few universities in this country that are this large. *Large* universities are those whose student body is between 25,000 and 50,000 students; there are a good number of these, typically the flagship (that is, main) campus of state universities. *Middle size* universities are those between 10,000 and 25,000 students; many, many universities fall into this category. *Smaller* universities are those with between 5,000 and 10,000 students; many colleges fall into this category. *Small* colleges have between 3,000 and 5,000 students, and *ultra-small* colleges are those that have fewer than 3,000 students (there are a few of these).

The larger the university or college is, the more likely it is that you'll have lots of majors, a broad variety of social activities, and many different kinds of students. On the other hand, you'll probably find larger classes (especially in the lower division, that is, first two years) and sometimes wait-lists to get into classes; a bureaucracy that rivals that of the DMV on a bad day; and, for some students, a feeling of anonymity. Smaller colleges will typically provide smaller classes, more opportunities to interact with the professors, quieter campus settings, and fewer activities. On the other hand, smaller colleges can also lack access to more sophisticated research equipment, for example in the sciences, and might offer fewer majors or a more limited course offering than their larger brethren (if you're doing very advanced or sophisticated work in some field you might run out of courses and have to take them at a neighboring college—sometimes a good idea, sometimes not so hot).

5-STAR TIP. The smaller the school you're considering, the more carefully you need to check out whether they offer the subjects you want to study. You might not find chiropterology (the study of bats), Akkadian (an ancient Semitic language), or ethnoarcheology (the study of contemporary cultures in an effort to interpret an archeological site) at a small or ultra-small college.

5. General versus special focus. Most colleges and universities in this country are broad-based, all-purpose schools that offer a wide variety of subjects in which you can take courses. But there are also a number of "special-" or "single-focus" schools, that is, institutions in which over 75 percent of the students are studying some particular subject. Some examples include arts schools (in which students might study painting, sculpture, or visual design); music conservatories (in which students study performance or composition); STEM schools (in which students concentrate on science, technology, engineering, or math); military academies (in which you might train to be an officer in one of the services); and a number of others. In addition, there are single-sex colleges (in which you'll find only men or women but not both); colleges that have a religious affiliation (though usually you need not be a practicing member of that religion or even, in some cases, a member at all to attend); and special mission colleges (which include HBCU—historically black colleges and universities and HSI—Hispanic-serving institutions).

Pick any of these only if you're very sure you want to spend most of your time on the area of focus, and you want to be around other students with interests very similar to your own. And keep in mind that in most cases you could study a particular field both at a special-focus or a general-purpose college. For example, you could be a music major both at a music school or a regular college (though, of course, the instruction will be more focused at a dedicated music conservatory).

6. Highly selective vs. somewhat selective vs. not-at-all selective. Some schools admit only a very small percentage of the applicants and have classes composed almost entirely of students with top grades in high school and very high SAT or ACT scores (along with other impressive accomplishments). Others admit students with a wider range of academic achievements and of standardized tests scores. And still others take all students who have completed a high school degree with a specified list of courses. In general, highly selective schools tend to have much more of an academic focus: the courses and assignments will be more demanding, students spend most of their time on academic pursuits, the students are more likely to show up at class fully prepared, and the students will do more of their work outside of class. Less selective schools might have an increased focus on social activities and, to some degree, as a consequence, less emphasis on academics: the courses generally are pitched to be accessible to a wider level of student abilities, and it will be far easier here to find students who blow off class or show up for quizzes totally unprepared. Finally, at a not-at-all selective school (including an open admissions school), the students will be representative of the college population as a whole: some students are very motivated, other less so, and still others not at all.

⑧ Things That Make Better Schools Better

Pretty early on in your college search you're likely to realize that some schools are the rock stars of the college scene. There's a buzz at your high school when their reps show up to give presentations. There's excitement and huge crowds around their tables at the college fairs. Some of your classmates become starry-eyed when their names come up. You know someone really smart who went there. But you might wonder: What's so great about these schools? Is what these schools have to offer so much better than what might be found at other, less talked-about colleges? Ultimately, the best college for you is going to be the one that's the best fit in a variety of areas: educational, social, financial, and many others. But on the educational side of things, as you start scoping out the college scene, you'll be better able to assess the offerings of any college you might be considering if you know about the academic features that distinguish the top-of-the-line colleges.

1. The faculty teach the classes. You would have thought that at every college it's the professors who teach the classes. Wrong. At many schools—in addition to the regular faculty that is composed of assistant, associate, and full professors—there is a cadre of lecturers, adjuncts, and graduate students who are hired to teach courses that, for whatever reason, the regular faculty doesn't want to teach (usually introductory or large lecture courses). Now we're not saying that every non-regular faculty member is bad, just that they're usually not as committed to the institution and its students (especially adjuncts teaching at many colleges); sometimes not as experienced (especially graduate students who might be teaching for the first time); and generally not required to do research (hence the teaching is more likely to be from the textbook rather than from their own research).

5-STAR TIP. To find out what percentage of courses are taught by non-regular faculty compare the *schedule of classes*, available on the web (which usually lists the names of the people teaching the courses that semester) with the list of departmental faculty, available on each department's web page (which lists all the regular faculty members). Courses with no faculty listed on the schedule are often courses taught by non-regular faculty, sometimes hired at the last minute.

BEST-KEPT SECRET. At schools that employ a large number of graduate students, there are usually rules about when graduate students are allowed to teach their own course (as opposed to leading discussion sections or doing just the grading). Better schools require a master's degree, or two to four years of graduate courses, or a year-long apprenticeship; less good (and more financially strapped) schools allow grad students to teach their own course their very first year of graduate school, often with no special training. Find out what is required at any school you're considering attending. Ask.

2. The professors do research. You might have thought that there was a sharp divide between teaching and research and that whatever obscure research the professor might be doing has no bearing on the course you might be taking from him or her. But that's not really the case. Professors who are used to doing creative and original work are more likely to ask *you* to do original and creative work, rather than just master the textbook or learn lots of little facts (indeed, some professors might have you study current articles in the fields, not just textbooks). Also, the fact that the professor does research will become more important in more advanced or upper division courses, in which the professor's being "up" on the goings on in his or her field—not to mention his or her own research in the field—can greatly influence the quality, and the currency, of the material you're being taught. And, at many top schools, advanced undergraduates can have the opportunity to work with the professors on the professors' research projects, even coauthoring articles in some cases—something you can't do if your prof isn't actually engaged in research.

5-STAR TIP. Some major research universities have groups of faculty concentrating on some issue or topic within their field—for instance, computational biology, physical applied mathematics, or cognitive and brain science—and have undergraduate courses to go with it. If you're applying to such schools, be on the lookout for such "groups."

3. The classes are smaller. There's a big difference between sitting in a lecture with 350 (or 550 or 750) students and a small class with only 20 or 25 students. In the first, you typically sit back like a sponge, passively absorbing and writing down what the professor has to say. In the second, you can have a two-way human interaction, where the professor knows the students, engages them in class discussion (which generally is a more effective way to learn than by listening to a lecture), and offers a variety of out-of-the-classroom learning experiences. To see what the size of classes is at schools you're considering, check the enrollment column in the college's schedule of classes or just ask some student.

EXTRA POINTER. As part of its rankings, *US News & World Report* includes information on percentage of classes under 20 students and percentage of classes over 50 students. Also, check out the student-to-faculty ratio: the smaller the ratio, the more likely it is you'll have small classes.

4. The instruction is on a higher level. You might have thought Physics 101 is the same at every school. Not so. At the better schools the material is presented on a higher level—often at a faster pace, with more emphasis on analysis and theory, and with less memorization (depending on the field). And there can be fewer tests and quizzes (the professor expects the students to master the basic "vocabulary" of the course without having to be tested on it), and more papers, studies, or projects. Also, in skills-based courses—math, physics and chemistry, world languages, and many other fields—there can be tiered courses, that is, many different levels of the same course, thus affording you an opportunity to take a more advanced version of the course if you have the relevant background, interest, or major.

5. The students are better—and work harder. Being among stronger and more motivated students—rather than among scores of slackers—helps motivate you to engage more fully with your classes and makes class discussions more lively, collaborative projects more fruitful, and study groups more helpful. Plus, it enables professors to offer more state-of-the-art and challenging courses. Professors have to tailor their classes to the level and ability of the students. So, at better schools you'll get classes that haven't been tamped down to accommodate lower levels of students' ability and motivation.

6. There are fewer requirements—and more ways to satisfy them. One mark of a less good school is that there is an exact list of distribution classes that everyone has to take and no one can place out of. What's bad about this is that, no matter what your level is, you're stuck with the same basic level (or, as it's called in the trade, "service") course that everyone has to take. Even if you are fine with taking that class, you're likely to find lots and lots of students who aren't; their bad attitude tends to drag down the whole class experience. Now add into the equation a professor bummed out by having to teach lots of students who don't want to be there and have no interest in the subject matter—and a professor who knows that the class has to be structured so that everyone, more or less, can pass the course.

Much better is the structure in which either there aren't so many requirements or where the requirements are grouped in *areas* and there are a good number of courses that satisfy each area requirement. Check the college and the departmental websites to see what's required at your choices of schools.

EXTRA POINTER. In some disciplines—for example, various kinds of engineering, music, world languages, and other fields—there's an exact four- or five-year program at every school. In these fields, a program of specifically required courses is not a negative. Also, at some schools there is a required first-year program, for example, a humanities or a "great books" sequence that is taught at a very high level—an exception, then, to the above generalization.

7. The curriculum is more sophisticated. Better schools generally offer a wide range of *majors* and *minors*, including subjects you wouldn't find in your high school, for instance, nanotechnology, international relations, oncology nursing, or Pashto. You're also likely to find many interdisciplinary *programs* (collections of courses from different departments or from different colleges within the university), such as Southeast Asian studies, religion, medieval and renaissance studies, logistics and transportation, and many, many others; and many *concentrations* (groupings of courses within a single department), for example, legal philosophy or behavioral economics.

8. The educational facilities are better. Not all schools are equally well capitalized (or, in street language, have equal amounts of money). As a result, not all schools have equally good facilities, for example, science labs and equipment, computer facilities, libraries, or other high-priced items. The leading universities generally offer top-level facilities, such as a particle accelerator (for physics), spectrometer (for optics), or a 3D printer (for art or engineering). If your interests turn you in a particular, equipment-driven direction, make sure the schools you're considering have what's needed for you to fulfill your dream.

2 BUILDING THE LIST

One of the major to-do's in the college application process is developing the list of schools to which you'll be applying. This is actually a pretty long-term process, which often involves many changes: additions, deletions, re-additions of deletions, and lots of back and forth. Don't worry if the formulation of your list doesn't happen all at once or in a linear fashion. It's likely that as you go through the process and learn more about both yourself and the colleges, some of your early ideas will fall by the wayside and new priorities will emerge. No problem. It doesn't matter if the journey is somewhat meandering as long as you reach a good destination.

At this point, you're still at the beginning of the journey so don't rush things. Right now is the time to gather information, not with the aim of narrowing things down but rather of expanding your possibilities. This is the time to experiment and try out alternatives that you might not have considered. You have a huge range of college options. So just as you might do in making any purchase in a big, well-stocked store, try on lots of different things—even things that you might not think are your style or will fit. If they end up not fitting, well that's OK, since at least you then know they're not for you. But maybe something you thought wouldn't fit actually looks good on you. And now you know more, too. It's all good.

This chapter will help you with your first stabs at formulating a list by giving you:

▶ 10 tips for making your initial list

▶ The top 12 websites to help you construct your initial list

▶ The top 10 websites for finding scholarships

▶ Tips and techniques for surfing the college websites

▶ 11 tips for going to see your college counselor

▶ Top 10 ways to make the most of the college night (or college rep visit)

▶ Do's and don'ts for attending college fairs

▶ E-mail etiquette

▶ Tips for avoiding the 10 biggest financial aid mistakes

▶ 10 questions to ask if you're considering Early Decision or Early Action

10 Tips for Making Your Initial List

With more than 4,000 colleges to choose from, many students feel pressure to settle on a few choices as soon as possible. *The sooner I get this list down to three or four*, they think, *the better*. But, in truth, this isn't the best strategy. At this stage in the process (which for many students is at the beginning of their junior year) it's much better to assemble a pretty good-sized list (ten to twenty entries wouldn't be too many), and then refine the list as you get more data. How the final list of colleges you apply to turns out depends in no small measure on which colleges are on the initial list. Follow our ten best tips and you'll have an excellent list to build on.

1. Cast the net widely. Don't assume that there necessarily is only one type of college that will satisfy your needs and interests. Someone interested in music might do just fine not only at a music conservatory but also at a liberal arts college with a good music program, a big state university with a famous marching band, or even a college with a limited music program but lots of music-making opportunities in the community. So, too, you might find that your interest in life in the big city could be satisfied not just at big city schools but also at more bucolic schools that are an easy commute to the bright lights.

2. Figure out what matters to you in a college. Although there's no need to have an exact list of your priorities, you should be starting to try to locate some key characteristics of schools that appeal to you. Are academics and the availability of particular majors especially important? How important are things such as location, weather, campus life, facilities, the "look and feel" of the campus, or the school's mission or social values? Will your religious affiliation affect your selection? Use our "10 Questions to Ask Yourself as You Begin Your College Search" (in chapter 1) to help you identify those factors that are most critical to you in your choice of colleges.

EXTRA POINTER. Know what your deal breakers are (most people have some). There's no point putting a single-sex college or a school 3,000 miles from home on your list if you already know that you absolutely, positively, 100 percent wouldn't go to a school like that, even if it were the last one on the planet.

 5-STAR TIP. Don't start your search looking for "the one." For any given person, there are any number of schools that will provide a wonderful college experience and there's no one school that will actually be a perfect fit.

3. Use the resources: both web and flesh and blood. As you start to populate your initial list, consider all sources of information, both virtual and real. If you know some living, breathing human beings who've been to college recently (or are now at college), poll them about the colleges they considered, which one they picked and why, and how they liked the one they went to (make sure to ask about the good, the bad, and the ugly—you want a complete picture). Then follow up by surfing the colleges' own websites and other general-purpose websites that might include videos as well as traditional e-content (consult our section "Top 12 Websites to Help You Construct Your Initial List," for some good sites). And prepare to get even more ideas from the various events that await you: the meeting with your high school counselor, college fairs and college nights, visits to the colleges, and even interviews with admissions professionals (all of these topics are discussed in sections to come shortly.)

4. Generate relevant alternatives. Many students start out with a very sparse list of names of colleges, maybe even only one or two choices. This is not necessarily a bad strategy, especially if the schools embody the characteristics you're looking for in a school (see tip 2 above). There are many ways to move from a single "focal" college to schools with similar features. One good way is simple word of mouth: find some student, perhaps a recent graduate of your school or a friend's older brother or sister, who got into the school you're considering and ask what other schools they applied to with the same characteristics.

BEST-KEPT SECRET. Best-Kept Secret. A more scientific, and extremely useful, way of finding alternatives is to use the website College Results Online. Go to WWW.COLLEGERESULTS.ORG/ SEARCH_BASIC.ASPX, click on the tab "Similar Colleges," and you'll be presented with ten to fifteen alternatives to the school you've inputted—some of which you might not have thought of or even heard of (for those in the latter class, navigate to those colleges' websites and see what the school is all about).

5. Don't overshoot—or undershoot. As you learn more about the college-selection process, you'll discover the sad fact that some schools have far, far more qualified candidates than they have places for—at some of the very best schools, as many as twenty times. Although you may have a straight-A average, excellent standardized test scores, and lots of extracurricular activities, you may not realize just how many other students around the country (and, gasp, in other countries) also have qualifications that match or exceed yours. On the other hand, if you have a strong record, don't just play it safe by applying to the less competitive schools that most everyone in your class applies to. Your final list will to need to have some variety in degree of selectivity, so make sure there's some variety in your initial list.

EXTRA POINTER. Don't take the numbers the colleges put out—twenty, thirty, even sixty thousand applicants—too seriously. Many colleges, in an attempt to build up their "brand," actively solicit applications from many, many students—not all of whom have even the minimum qualifications for getting into that school. A seven percent chance of getting in makes sense only if you know the pool of applicants—and how many are nonstarters (something the colleges never let on).

REALITY CHECK. Disregard comments such as "it's all a crapshoot" or "you'd be better buying a lottery ticket than applying to that school." There's some rhyme or reason to the selection process, and even at the selective schools 6 to 10 percent of the applicants get in (when was the last time you bought a lottery ticket with a one-in-fifteen or a one-in-ten chance of winning the grand prize?).

EXTRA POINTER. A number of websites provide statistical analysis of the typical entering class (see the section "Top 12 Websites to Help You Construct Your Initial List"). Pay special attention to the SAT/ACT 25th to 75th percentile range of recent admits. That'll give you a rough-and-ready idea of where you stand relative to recent admits (of course the complete admissions procedure is much more complicated, but still ...).

6. Start thinking about the finances. Although it's not yet time to raid your and your parents' savings, it is time to give some preliminary thought to what four or five years of college are going to cost you. If, as it is for the majority of college students, financial aid is going to be factor, then you should pay some attention to cost in making your initial list. But beware. Some seemingly expensive private colleges have large endowments and can provide very generous financial aid—sometimes even more than state universities, especially out-of-state state universities. (See our "The 10 Biggest Financial Aid Mistakes—and How to Avoid Them" for more on this.) In addition, many community and city colleges, and some state universities (if you're in-state) can be incredibly cheap (some states have lottery funds dedicated to subventing your college tuition or offer generous aid to academically accomplished students), so don't assume that just because it's a state school that it has no money to offer.

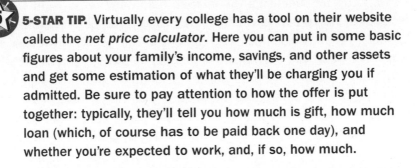

5-STAR TIP. Virtually every college has a tool on their website called the *net price calculator*. Here you can put in some basic figures about your family's income, savings, and other assets and get some estimation of what they'll be charging you if admitted. Be sure to pay attention to how the offer is put together: typically, they'll tell you how much is gift, how much loan (which, of course has to be paid back one day), and whether you're expected to work, and, if so, how much.

7. Get input from your high school counselor. These days college admissions statistics are important to the reputation of a high school, so many college counselors are quite knowledgeable about the college scene. Even better, if they know you and have some sense of your individual interests and talents, they can come up with names of colleges that you might not be familiar with but that would be great choices for you. Also, some counselors know of colleges—sometimes in the region, sometimes not—that are especially generous with financial aid or simply are good values. Keep in mind, though, that some counselors may be less helpful than others, especially ones who have developed an artificially narrow range of schools they recommend to students—maybe they limit their suggestions to colleges in the area or to schools that others at your school have attended. (To make the most of your meeting with the counselor see "11 Tips for Going to See Your College Counselor.")

EXTRA POINTER. As you move forward on the college search, new schools will occur to you to consider. Run these by your counselor. Many high school counselors welcome additional visits from students looking at colleges and, as a bonus, they'll know you better when it comes time for them to write a letter of recommendation for your application.

8. Keep the "rankings" in perspective. Many colleges, in an attempt to woo prospective students, proudly trumpet their rankings, especially those published by *US News & World Report* (www.usnews .com/education). Although these rankings can provide some useful information, keep in mind that minor differences in the rankings don't reflect significant differences in the quality of the schools: a school that ranks a few points down from another really isn't in any significant way worse than the one a few points up on the ladder. Also realize, first, that a significant portion of the data can be gamed by the colleges—they can admit slightly better students just to get in the top 50 or they can solicit alumni donations just by asking everyone to contribute a few bucks; second, that some of the data comes from people not actually teaching at colleges (college presidents, for example, are often primarily fundraisers, not professors); and third, that high school counselors (now included in evaluating the school's reputation) in many cases are not familiar with all that many colleges (and can favor colleges in their region, not necessarily the best schools).

9. Deal in all the "stakeholders." Whether you like it or not, your parents (and, in some families, also grandparents or other relatives) are going to have a big say in where you end up going to college—especially if they'll be the ones footing the bill. So it's a good idea to hear their ideas about possible schools and add some of them into the mix (especially if their choices strike you as reasonable). That said, you don't have to swallow what everyone else tells you if it doesn't match your personal goals and interests—and even worse, if it falls into the category of deal breaker. At the end of the day, you're the one who's going to have to go to the school, so you might as well construct your initial list with that in mind.

10. Keep it fluid. Names of colleges will be added and deleted from the initial list as the process continues and you gain more and more sense of the colleges you're considering. Don't feel that your initial list is set in stone and that it's some kind of no-no to change your mind. Eventually you will need to narrow your choices and firm up your decisions. But not now.

Top 12 Websites to Help You Construct Your Initial List

A Google search for "college websites" returns 335,000,000 hits; a search for "picking a college," 13,400,000. Talk about information overload. How's anyone supposed to find any useful information to help them compose their initial list of colleges? To help you narrow your search, here is a list of our dozen favorite all-purpose college websites.

1. Big Future: **HTTPS://BIGFUTURE.COLLEGEBOARD.ORG/**

This comprehensive site powered by The College Board should be every college-seeking student's first stop on the web. In addition to helpful information about finding colleges, paying for college, and an interactive making-a-plan engine, the site includes information about majors and careers and how to find one that's right for you. While you're there, you can also register for SAT and AP tests.

2. College Compass: **WWW.USNEWS.COM/USNEWS/STORE/COLLEGE_ COMPASS.HTM**

This is the *US News & World Report*'s premium tier and hence the only site on this list that you'll have to pay for (about $30 a year). But, in addition to the complete rankings (which are free to anyone), it offers a tool that'll enable you to put in twenty-three filters, which will then generate a list of colleges they think are appropriate for you (very good if you're short on ideas of how to populate your list). It also includes a wealth of information about admission standards, financial aid, college life, and sports programs.

3. NACAC: **WWW.NACACNET.ORG/STUDENTINFO/PAGES/DEFAULT.ASPX**

The National Association of College Admission Counselors offers loads of information in one site, including tips for college prep, a college search engine, advice about applications, and information about paying for college and succeeding in college. You'll also find a complete schedule of college fairs (for more on College Fairs, see the section "Do's and Don'ts for Attending College Fairs"), links to various rankings (can be useful, if kept in proper perspective), as well as interesting reports on various issues in the college-application process (stimulating reading for those who want to delve deeper into some issue).

4. Unigo: HTTPS://WWW.UNIGO.COM/

The brainchild of Jordan Goldman, Unigo is the first twenty-first-century-ready college website. Combining student reviews with actual student videos, Unigo offers a real-time glance at the "look and feel" of over one thousand colleges. An excellent choice for learning about colleges you're not able to visit in person, Unigo should be a part of every student's college search. Similar to any user-generated content site, though, be sure to tread carefully; opinions can vary widely, and you shouldn't use one student's negative comments to rule out a college.

EXTRA POINTER. If you like Unigo, you also might like College Click TV: WWW.COLLEGECLICKTV.COM. Here you'll find student-submitted videos, complete with tags (very helpful for searching out specific aspects of campus, such as student body, spirit, professors, and even tailgating). Again, it's the good, the bad, and the ugly—so be sure to look at lots of videos. Also recommended: WWW.ECAMPUSTOURS.COM, which offers virtual panoramic tours of more than 1,300 campuses.

5. Niche: HTTP://NICHE.COM/

This unusual site (formerly College Prowler) ranks colleges in thirty-plus categories, including "best social scene," "campus strictness," and "if I could do it all over again." A very useful complement to Unigo and College Click TV, it includes thousands of student reviews, organized by categories. Check out special features such as "frequently compared" (similar schools, each with their own rankings), "students often come from" (high schools from which many students come), and "campus tour" (informative videos, though be careful, the schools often have a big share in the content presentations).

6. The University of Illinois's College and University Rankings: **www .LIBRARY.UIUC.EDU/EDX/RANKINGS.HTM**

The University of Illinois at Urbana-Champaign gives an informative overview of various ranking services, including a master list of more than twenty different rating services (complete with URLs). These range from well-known favorites—such as, *US News & World Report, Forbes, Kiplinger*'s, and *Princeton Review*—to lesser-known sites— such as Parchment, Students Review, College Factual, Asian Nation's Best Colleges for Asian Americans, and Black Enterprise's Top Colleges for African Americans. An excellent and useful meta-site on college rankings thanks to the nice folks at U of I.

7. Fair Test: **WWW.FAIRTEST.ORG**

Bombed the ACT or SAT? Or think that standardized testing doesn't really measure anything important? Then you'll like Fair Test, the site of the National Center for Fair and Open Testing. Their mission is to try to end the misuse or overuse of standardized testing, so its website includes a list of more than eight hundred colleges and universities that have flexible or optional standardized testing requirements. Fun to look at even if you have awesome test scores.

8. The Alumni Factor: **HTTPS://WWW.ALUMNIFACTOR.COM/**

This new entry in the college admissions arena ranks colleges from the other end: it focuses on how well students do after they graduate, rather than on how accomplished they are coming in. The rankings here are based on factors such as intellectual, social, and spiritual development, as well as, of course, career success (very important these days). You can actually customize the ranking formula (which is applied to 227 schools) by adjusting the weighting to reflect how important (or not) each of the rating factors is for you.

9. College Data: WWW.COLLEGEDATA.COM

This beast of a site provides a wealth of information about admission, money matters (including tuition, profile of financial aid recipients, and financial aid programs), academics (including majors, gen ed requirements, faculty, and AP policies), and campus life (including weather, housing, security, sports, and student activities). Also available is a college admissions tracker—see how you compare to real students who got in and calculate your chances of following in their footsteps—and a net price calculator—get a rough idea of how much each of these colleges is going to cost you.

ON THE WEB. For data seeking techies, College Navigator HTTP://NCES.ED.GOV/COLLEGENAVIGATOR, run by the National Council of Education Statistics, and College Insight HTTP://COLLEGE-INSIGHT.ORG/ provide entertaining reading.

And many will enjoy Parchment WWW.PARCHMENT.COM, where not only can you search out colleges right for you but also you can use their user-submitted results to gauge your chances of getting in to the college of your choice (of course, there are no guarantees…).

Good tools are also available at College Reality Check HTTPS://COLLEGEREALITYCHECK.COM, an informative and newsy site run by the Chronicle of Higher Education.

10. College Results Online: WWW.COLLEGERESULTS.ORG

An incredibly useful site, College Results Online gathers data from a wide variety of sources (including federal, state, and private databases) and enables you to find relevant and informed alternatives to the college you might have your eye on. An invaluable tool in generating your initial list of colleges.

11. Common Data Set

To find, search "common data set" plus the name of the individual college you're looking at (not available for all colleges). An intriguing and unbelievably revealing source of information, in which the colleges themselves give their own data on a multitude of issues, including what factors they consider in admissions; the number of students admitted in each "band" of SAT and ACT scores (700–800, 600–699, etc.); the percentage of admits in each tier of class rank (top 10 percent, top 25 percent, etc.); what types of financial aid are offered and what the average award is; and much, much more. Also includes information about instructional programs, class sizes, and general student life.

 5-STAR TIP. Be sure to focus on section C of the Common Data Set: that's where the most useful information about how they actually pick is contained.

12. College Confidential: WWW.COLLEGECONFIDENTIAL.COM

If you haven't already heard of this site in your college search, you will. Most noteworthy here is the "web's busiest discussion community" (if they do say so themselves). Some of the threads here are unpleasantly angst-filled and some have misinformation and rumor, but others have answers from people who've either "been there, done that" or who are particularly knowledgeable about the topic you're interested in. Just stay away from this site around college notification days (both early and regular decision). You won't welcome the very stressful, minute-by-minute posts of where people got in, where they got deferred, or where they got axed.

Bonus Sites. Know How 2 GO: WWW.KNOWHOW2GO.ORG and You Can Go: WWW.YOUCANGO.COLLEGEBOARD.ORG.

A public service initiative sponsored by the American Council on Education, the Lumina Foundation, and the Ad Council, Know How 2 GO offers college information in English, Spanish, Arabic, and Hmong!—and special information for members of the military and veterans. You Can Go, an initiative of the College Board, offers success stories about students preparing, applying to, and paying for college. Both sites are well worth a look.

Top 10 Websites for Finding Scholarships

One of the most important parts of many students' search is finding the money to pay for it—and much of the successful searching is done on the web. So we invited financial aid guru Mark Kantrowitz, senior vice president and publisher of EDVISORS.COM, to share his very best ideas. Here's what he recommends.

According to Google, there are more than 87.5 million web pages that mention the word "scholarships" and 156 million that mention the word "scholarship." While it can be helpful to search for narrowly specified types of scholarships, such as "Coca-Cola scholarships," there are also many websites that match the student's personal background profile against a large database of scholarships, making it easier to find scholarships for which you are eligible.

Here is a list of the best free scholarship-matching services and compilations of top scholarships. Search at least two of these sites to be sure to find all of the scholarships for which you are qualified:

1. Fastweb: WWW.FASTWEB.COM

Fastweb was the first free scholarship-matching service, and remains the most popular. It will alert you to new scholarships and upcoming deadlines by e-mail.

2. Student Scholarship Search: WWW.STUDENTSCHOLARSHIPSEARCH.COM

Not only will Student Scholarship Search match students against a database of scholarships but also students can compile and share their own curated lists of scholarships.

3. Big Future: WWW.BIGFUTURE.COLLEGEBOARD.ORG

The College Board publishes a free scholarship search tool listing more than 2,200 programs that participate in the College Board's annual survey of financial aid programs. An excellent place to start.

4. Merit Aid: **WWW.MERITAID.COM**

Meritaid.com provides a specialized database of merit-based scholarships (that is, scholarships based wholly on academic achievements and promise, not financial need) offered by colleges and universities to recruit talented students.

5. Scholarship Points: **WWW.SCHOLARSHIPPOINTS.COM**

Students can earn points by completing activities, such as answering surveys, and use the points to enter random drawings for scholarships. To date, the website has given away more than $750,000 in free college scholarships.

6. Peterson's: **WWW.PETERSONS.COM**

Petersons started off as a college guide publisher. Now owned by Nelnet, a diversified education lender and servicer, Petersons still publishes a free database of thousands of scholarships.

7. College Data: **WWW.COLLEGEDATA.COM**

College Data, owned by 1st Financial Bank, licenses college search and scholarship search data to other websites. You can also search their databases on their own website.

8. Scholarships.com: **WWW.SCHOLARSHIPS.COM**

Scholarships.com appears at the top of search results for "scholarships" because it has the right domain name.

9. Edvisors: **WWW.EDVISORS.COM/SCHOLARSHIPS**

Edvisors.com publishes numerous specialized lists of scholarships, such as the most prestigious scholarships, most generous scholarships, quirky and unusual scholarships, most popular scholarships, community college scholarships, easy scholarships, and scholarships for students under age thirteen, among numerous others.

10. Scholarship Experts: **WWW.SCHOLARSHIPEXPERTS.COM**

Yet another scholarship-matching service. Similar to the others, ScholarshipExperts.com claims to have the largest number of scholarships.

Surfing the College Website: Tips and Techniques

One of the best resources for students thinking about college is the college website. Here you'll learn about the most distinctive features of each college—or at least what each college would like you to think are its best features. No matter. With some skillful surfing, you'll be able to uncover the underbelly of the beast you're about to spend the next four (or more) years of your life in. Here's how:

1. Start with the "About." Every college has an **ABOUT** tab somewhere on its main home page. Here you'll find the most basic information about the college: its goals and mission, its history, programs and departments it's especially proud of, the composition of its student body, and sometimes even how it got its name. Having this information will give you the big picture of what the college is about and, important, will help you eliminate colleges that for whatever reason are not right for you.

2. Tab to the tabs. Once you have a broad overview of the college, the next thing to do is explore other tabs that are relevant to potential students (i.e., you). Ones especially to consider include **ADMISSIONS**, **ACADEMICS**, **RESEARCH**, and **CAMPUS LIFE**. Also, be on the lookout for tabs for both **PROSPECTIVE** (or **FUTURE**) **STUDENTS** and **CURRENT STUDENTS**. Sometimes there's much better information for those already at the college than for those thinking they might like to go there.

 BEST-KEPT SECRET. Some colleges, especially multidivisional universities, have separate web pages for each of their individual colleges or schools, such as liberal arts, engineering, business, architecture, performing arts, nursing, hotel management, and so on. Sometimes these are buried under **ACADEMICS** or **UNDERGRADUATE EDUCATION**. But with a little bit of digging you ought to be able to unearth these important, and often very informative, subpages. Well worth the effort.

EPIC FAIL! Be sure you don't mistake a graduate program for an undergraduate school or college. You wouldn't want to pick a school only to find out that the program in "health sciences and medicine" is only for students who already have a BA in chemistry.

3. Scour the admissions area. Here you'll find out essential matters about the admissions requirements, application procedures, deadlines, and that all-important info about financial aid. You'll be able to guess if you can get in and, once in, whether you'll be able to afford to stay.

5-STAR TIP. As you're navigating the admissions section, be sure to take careful notes about the particularities of the school you're visiting—notes that you can read afterward (electronic note taking is good this way). It's a bad moment when, after surfing twenty-five colleges, you can't remember which one offers the John R. Hoofalus full scholarship—given only to students with just your last name.

4. Scope out the "extras." Take a peek at the special programs at the college—for example, the first-year experience (FYE) course or freshman seminar (FS), the honors college, the study-abroad program, and any community service ("service learning") and internship opportunities. These differ widely from college to college and can be a good gauge of the mission and focus of the college, as well as of how many bucks it has to spend on such programs. And although these might seem like extras, they could be some of the most valuable educational experiences you're going to have at college.

EXTRA POINTER. And while you're at it, how about the free services provided: the writing center, the academic advancement center, the tutoring service, the health services and counseling center, and the center for students with disabilities? All of these could be valuable to you and could be a measure of how committed to student support the college is.

5. Bone up on the requirements. Many colleges have a number of courses that you are required to take—sometimes called core courses or general education ("gen ed") requirements. And if that weren't enough, there are distribution requirements—different areas of study (for example, humanities, social science, science) in which you have to take a specified number of classes. Carefully consider how many such courses there are and how restrictive a college program you're buying into. And be aware that some colleges have specific must-do courses that everyone must take, while others have only general area, or methods of learning, requirements that many courses will satisfy.

REALITY CHECK. While you're thinking about requirements, it's worth checking up to see whether you can use AP or IB courses to place out of some of the requirements, and whether you can substitute a higher-level course for the one-size-fits-all class in some field you've already taken four courses in. Placing out of some gen ed requirements can free some time in your first year to take some things you're really interested in—making for a more pleasant college experience.

6. Check out the majors. Some schools might only have about 20 majors, while others can list as many as 354. So, especially if you have a field you think you'd like to learn about, it's important to check to see that the college actually teaches that area. You'd be amazed at how often some hapless student arrives at college only to find that it doesn't have the major he or she planned on taking.

BEST-KEPT SECRET. And while you're thinking about majors, it'd be a good idea to click on the link for the department (or departmental) home page for that major. There you'll find a list of requirements for that major, a list of the faculty members who teach in that major, and with any luck, some course pages with actual syllabuses. Check out what the faculty teach and what they think about in their research (often contained in individual web pages).

7. Cruise the course schedule. Colleges have two kinds of listings for the courses taught. One is the course *catalog*, which lists every possible course offered at the school—a sort of history of all courses that have ever been taught and a hope chest for ones that might be taught. The other is the course *schedule*—a listing of the courses actually offered in a given semester (e.g., fall 2015, winter 2016). Concentrate on the course *schedule*. Ask yourself, how many courses are being taught, how big are the courses, how many hours a week do they meet, and are they lectures or discussions (or both)? (If you can't immediately find the course schedule, use the search box, usually located at the top right of the page, to search for *Schedule of Classes*, *Course Schedule*, or *Courses Offered <semester, year>*.)

EXTRA POINTER. At some schools, the course schedule is password protected. If you can't get to the course schedule, wait till you visit the campus then ask a student if he or she will log in to let you see the course schedule. (Promise them you won't peek at their grades and personal e-mail. Or maybe your accomplice can watch over your shoulder while you peruse the schedule.)

BEST-KEPT SECRET. At some schools, there are links from each course listing to the syllabus and books for that course. Use these to see what's actually taught in that course.

8. Assess the atmosphere. Colleges have met YouTube, so at many college websites you'll find professional-level videos offering you "tours of the campus." These videos will give you a pretty good idea of the things the school wants to highlight—their shiny new buildings, modern labs, inviting dorms, lovely student center, ginormous football stadium, beautifully landscaped lawns, and gourmet offerings at the food court. Enjoy the tour, but take it with a healthy skepticism. Colleges never show you the overflowing toilets in the non–air conditioned dorms, the lectures with 700 people in them, and the buckets under the leaks in the up-for-demolition psych building.

9. Go clubbing. It's always nice to see what kinds of student clubs a college has, and there's usually something for every student, from the rock/paper/scissors club to the Death Cab for Cutie fan club. And, even if you don't want to join in on the fun, the information will give you a better feel for what's going on at the school and what the students are like.

10. Start the conversation. Make a note of any questions that occur to you while surfing the website, then e-mail them to the appropriate office—admissions, financial aid, the undergraduate advisor in a particular department, or even an individual professor or a student you might know. Many university folk are eager to reach out to potential students, and if no one answers your e-mail—well that's a fact about that school, too.

11 Tips for Going to See Your College Counselor

For many students, the visit to their college (or guidance) counselor is the first occasion to think about college in any serious way. *Wow*, some students think, *I'm actually going to have to do this college-application thing some time this year, or next, or the year after that*. But whether you're assigned a college counselor as a freshman, sophomore, or junior (junior year is most common), you should view your college counselor as an ally: depending on your school structure and the personality of the counselor him- or herself, the counselor is a combination of mentor, friend, advisor, sounding board, and co-navigator of your high school's bureaucracy. You'll have the best possible relations and the most productive meetings if you follow our top eleven tips for going to see your counselor.

1. Bring some ideas to the first meeting. You'll have the most productive meeting if you come in with a couple of "focal" colleges—colleges that you think you might be interested in going to. And pinpoint what about the colleges interests you: academic reputation, some major or program, a friend or relative who went there, proximity to home (or distance), or size (it's a giant U or a small college). Having even a few ideas in mind will help your counselor expand your list by proposing other colleges with similar features. And if you can't come up with any ideas, at least formulate a number of things you might be looking for in a college so that your counselor can begin to make suggestions tailored to your needs and preferences.

2. Bring your "brag sheet." Most college counselors see dozens—indeed, in some cases, hundreds—of students. So your counselor might not be all that familiar with your classwork, activities, or you as a person. Bring in a short list, perhaps bullet-pointed, highlighting particular achievements and activities that show you in your best light and establish you as a unique individual. Things you might include: any special classes you took and special projects you did in them; your extracurricular activities and any special leadership roles you played in them; any special activities (for example, work or service experiences) you did outside school and what you learned from them; any employment you've held or special family responsibilities you've had to take on; finally, anything distinctive about you that might help the counselor find colleges appropriate to you. And write it down: the very process of writing it down will help you focus your thoughts and get it all in mind for your meeting with the counselor.

BEST-KEPT SECRET. In most cases, your counselor will have to write a letter of recommendation for you to the colleges. Getting him or her some information about you and your record (even at the first meeting) will help him or her write a fuller—and more convincing—letter. And if your school provides a questionnaire, fill it out carefully. It, too, can function as a template for your counselor's letter of recommendation.

5-STAR TIP. Don't be too modest or downplay your achievements or awards in your list or brag sheet. You can always edit it down for the actual application, but at this point it's important to tell the full story to your counselor (he or she can make suggestions for tweaks later).

   3. Don't bring your parents (at least to the first meeting). What the counselor is most interested in is what you value in a college—not what your parents are looking for. Also, the counselor wants to get a better sense of you as a person—not what your parents think you are (or should be). Especially if your parents have been talking college 24/7 for the last two years, having them in attendance might overpower, or at least color, the conversation between you and the counselor. Upshot? Ditch the folks, at least for now.

EPIC FAIL! If you do decide to bring your parents (some schools encourage this) don't bring your family's dirty laundry or simmering sibling drama to the meeting. Your time together with your counselor should center on the college search, not devolve into family therapy. Your counselor will resist taking sides in family disputes, especially ones that step outside the bounds of college advising.

4. Keep a very open mind. Your college counselor will bring many resources to the table: experience with many students, like and unlike yourself; visits to colleges and meetings with admission reps and officials; and knowledge of many, many colleges, some of which you might have heard of and some of which you might not have. Take his or her suggestions seriously and probe what there is about that college that makes it right for you: Is your counselor just working off the *US News & World Report* rankings or does he or she know of some particular program at the college that fits your interests especially well? Is your counselor just picking three schools within 100 miles of your home or does he or she know that you'd feel most comfortable in a small school and knows schools that have an especially welcoming environment? Does your counselor know of financial aid opportunities either in the region or nationally? Whatever the suggestions, find out *why* they're suggestions for you.

5-STAR TIP. College counselors will typically offer you a range of college communities and styles that mirror your "focal colleges" (see tip 1) and then suggest ones that stretch the conception you've defined, moving further and further out of your comfort zone. Consider the suggestions, despite whatever resistance you might feel. Your counselor might know something of value (and besides, you're going to have to apply to a whole slew of colleges, not just two or three, so keep the suggestions as possibilities).

5. Be forthcoming. There's nothing college counselors hate more than students who offer up non-communicative, monosyllabic answers. "What sorts of colleges are you thinking of?"—"Dunno, haven't really thought about it." "Would you like a big or small school?"—"Either would be fine." If you're too reticent in the meeting or if you come off as not having thought about college at all, the counselor will not be able to provide any useful guidance, and, in the worst case, will try to get you out of the office and move onto to the next student. It's just human nature.

 5-STAR TIP. If you're not sure what to say about yourself, refer to the narrative you brought in with you (see tip 2 above).

 EXTRA POINTER. If your counselor asks you a question and you don't have any idea what the answer is, don't get flummoxed; simply say, "I don't know, I'll find out," then get back to him or her later.

6. But don't bare your soul. The college counseling session is meant to be a discussion about your college plans and possible colleges to apply to—not a therapy session. Even if you're feeling stressed or depressed, don't let your meeting degenerate into "I'm not really sure I want to go to college at all," "I've never really been good at anything, so how can I start now?" or "I don't really feel comfortable with who I am, so how can I present myself to a college?" These are all valid questions to be asking—just not at the first meeting with your college counselor. If you develop a relationship with your counselor later on, you can start to delve into more complex questions about college and your college life.

7. Don't be afraid to talk finances. For most students today, money is an issue in selecting a college—especially because college tuition has been rising at twice the pace of inflation for most of the last ten years. So if your choice in colleges will be influenced by how much it costs and the possibility of getting need- or merit-based financial aid, by all means point this out to the counselor. It is no shame not to be in the top 1 percent of income (99 percent of people aren't). Many college counselors know how much various colleges cost, and, more important, know colleges that offer large fellowships or especially good financial aid packages.

EXTRA POINTER. If you don't know your family's financial situation, go to your dad and mom and ask: "I'm going to see my counselor next Thursday, and I need to know whether we were expecting financial aid from college and how much of a factor that's going to be in our choice of colleges."

8. Never lock horns. As in any human interaction, communication failures sometimes occur in a counselor-student meeting. Perhaps you don't agree with your counselor's suggestions, feel that he or she is proposing schools not good enough for your brilliant intellectual abilities, or maybe you just don't like what you're hearing—or the counselor you're hearing it from. But relax. It's never a good idea to be contentious or unpleasant with your counselor. After all, you don't have to do what he or she says; you could apply to all or some of the colleges he or she is proposing—or none of them at all. And keep in mind that later in the process, the counselor is most likely going to have to write a recommendation for you, so it's a good idea not to piss him or her off.

REALITY CHECK. When real communication problems happen, they tend to come from some kind of misinformation. Your counselor may be missing important, emotional pieces of your college puzzle, or you might not fully understand a key component of an application process. If you are at an impasse and not communicating well, make a plan to come back a week later and pick it up again when you've had a chance to think, research, and chill out a bit.

9. Write it all down. Take careful notes of all the counselor's suggestions—and what's good about each. As you progress in the college quest, you'll be getting more and more information—much of which you won't be able to remember when you actually have to apply to the colleges. And keep in mind that many colleges will have common features, especially if you're applying to many colleges of a similar type, so be sure to note down what's different (or special or unusual) about each of the colleges mentioned.

10. Do further research. One of the best things you can do after you've had a (we hope productive) first meeting with your college counselor is to find out more about the particular colleges he or she has recommended. Go to their websites, scout them out; see how these colleges stack up against ones you have in mind; see if you can find someone who has actually attended those colleges in recent memory (nothing beats info straight from a horse's mouth).

11. Keep your counselor informed. Be sure to keep your counselor in the loop. New developments in your search, ACT or SAT scores that arrive, your own evolving thoughts, impressions from colleges you visit, things you hear from colleges, indeed simple questions and chit-chat—all of these will enrich the relation between you and your counselor and make the whole ongoing interaction more beneficial to you.

BONUS TIP. If after meeting your counselor a number of times you feel that you are not getting the help you need—or if adequate advising isn't available at your high school—you might consider an educational consultant or outside advisor. These professionals charge a range of costs, so be sure they offer sufficient value for the price they're charging. If you decide to go this route, it's best to hire someone who is certified, a member of IECA (Independent Educational Counselors Association) and a member of NACAC, the governing body for admission and counseling professionals. Most important, steer far clear of counselors who make lofty promises, hint at "calling in favors from admission friends," or state they "will get you in to your top choice(s)." Counselors are advisors, not magicians.

Top 10 Ways to Make the Most of the College Night (or College Rep Visit)

Colleges send out glossy brochures, design information-filled websites, and sometimes even advertise in magazines and on the web. But sometimes you need to hear what it's all about from a living, breathing human being. Enter the college rep. Admissions officers (or reps) travel in spring, fall, and sometimes summer to pitch the college to prospective students (i.e., you), answer your questions, and, in the best case, motivate you to apply to their college. Traditionally, the visit has been during the day, often at individual high schools (the so-called *college rep visit*, or at some schools, confusingly, *college visit*). But now, increasingly, the college reps are doubling (or tripling or quadrupling) up by offering an evening event for a number of high schools at a public library, convention center, or mall (the so-called *college night*). Sound intriguing? It will be, if you follow our ten best tips for making the most of the college night or visit.

1. Do the legwork. Colleges design their websites to answer basic questions and to give info about their citadel of learning. Take the time to familiarize yourself with the contours of the college before attending the event: information about things such as available majors, school requirements, application deadlines, testing requirements, and financial aid policies (see "Surfing the College Website: Tips and Techniques" for how best to do this). You'll want to be up on the basics so that you can focus on unobvious—and more valuable—features of the college being presented.

2. Be fashionably early. Admissions presentations have an on and an off time, and the best time to make a real connection is when the rep is off script. In many cases, it's good to come early and spend a few minutes chatting with the admissions officer before he or she starts the presentation (of course, if the rep seems nervous or busy, this might not be the best time, try after the presentation instead).

Keep the conversation casual. Most likely, you'll find the rep friendly and engaging. Best of all (if the group is small enough) he or she will remember you as taking the initiative to talk with him or her.

3. Learn the "admissions code." Admissions presentations communicate what the school values in an application. Pay careful attention to:

▶ whether the rep discusses SATs or ACTs at length (translation: we pay a lot of attention to standardized tests) or not so much (translation: we start our evaluation on other parts of the application)

▶ whether the rep emphasizes "campus involvement" or "community service" (translation: we like applications that showcase leadership and service activities)

▶ whether the rep talks about "academic achievement" and "intellectual focus" (translation: we want very high-achieving students)

▶ whether the rep says that interviews are not required, but "recommended" (translation: although we can't require an interview, it sure can help your application)

▶ whether the rep offers up anything that could help you construct a better application for that school (translation: I know what we're looking for because I actually read the applications or else have heard from my colleagues what they look for in an application).

 5-STAR TIP. Veteran admission reps love to help and they have experiences to share. Often you'll hear practical tips to spruce up your application such as essay topics to avoid, common missteps applicants make, or little known tips for admission. Bring your college notebook (or device) and jot down what you hear, preferably in the rep's exact words; it's likely you'll get a peek behind the curtain that you can't get anywhere else.

4. Learn the "culture code." Admissions presentations also communicate the school's own perception of itself. Does the video lead with the football stadium or the classroom? What gets the most air time during a discussion of campus life: Greek life, study abroad, collaboration with professors, freedom in choosing courses, the core curriculum, or the honor code? What's emphasized in—and what's left out of—the presentation gives you indicators of the school's culture, and after you've gone to a number of college nights you'll be able to locate what differentiates one college from another.

BEST-KEPT SECRET. Every college or university has campus annoyances or institutional shortcomings to deemphasize or outright hide. Be on the lookout. Colleges with many big classes might distract you with the student-to-faculty ratio instead of the percentage of classes under twenty students. An overhyped student activities list might reflect the fact that students flee campus on weekends and keeping them on campus is a priority for the dean's office. Excessive focus on the security of the campus might indicate there's a safety problem. All factors to consider.

5. Take it with a grain of salt. No matter how you slice it, it's the job of the rep to sell the school. And it's the job of the video—almost always a part of the college night or visit—to advertise the college. Listen to what they say, but adopt a healthy skepticism.

6. Speak up (you have a mouth). Every college night or college rep visit comes with a question period when you can ask anything you want to know about the presentation or the college generally. Is there such a thing as a stupid question? Yes and most often it's asking an admission rep something you could have looked up yourself. Don't be remembered as the "Let Me Google That for You" kid. Basic questions such as Are first-year students allowed cars on campus? Can I get college credit for my 3 in AP human geography? Can I major in drama? will have that admission rep scanning the audience for the next raised hand. Instead, ask questions that probe more interesting possibilities, that go more deeply into the college culture, or that only an insider could answer. For instance, What kinds of students do really well at your school? What are the strongest departments in your university? Is it possible to take courses from another college within the university for credit? Can one create one's own major?

 5-STAR TIP. In some cases the rep will make time for individual, private questions after his or her presentation. Make sure you avail yourself of this golden opportunity to ask questions that pertain to your goals, interests, or concerns about the college. No point asking about whether you'll get in, they won't tell. But you can ask a little about how to tweak you application or what features you have that might make you attractive to their college. The rep is a human being, too, and in most cases is willing to offer you some guidance in applying.

7. Be enthusiastic and engaging. If you do choose to talk to the rep, either before or after the presentation, you may be the first (or the last) of students he or she will meet that day, and that rep needs your energy. Look him or her in the eye, shake his or her hand, tell him or her you enjoyed the presentation (if your meeting is afterwards), ask how his or her travel is going, or otherwise communicate your enthusiasm to meet the rep. Everyone responds to a positive presence and an energetic soul, so bring your best, most engaging personality to the fore and you're sure to make a good impression.

8. Don't worry if you have to leave. Especially in the college rep visit case, don't feel bad if you have to leave early. Admission reps understand that you have to show up on time for classes and they won't count your early exit against you.

BEST-KEPT SECRET. Some colleges measure what they call "demonstrated interest" (that is, how eager you are to attend their school) by how many "points-of-contact" you have with that college and its officials. So if you're offered to fill out a contact card or to put your name and e-mail on some list, be sure to do it. There's no downside and at some colleges it could actually increase your chances of admission. And, if the rep offers his or her card, by all means take it: gives you the best way to reach the rep (and the contact point the school might be counting). Also, in the very best case, if the rep would like to talk with you in greater detail about your interests and activities, go for it! That's a golden expression of interest on the college's part.

REALITY CHECK. The reason some schools are interested in gauging how interested you are in going can be that they have low "yield"—that, for instance, only 30 percent of the people offered admission actually come to that school. So they figure (rightly or wrongly) that the applicants who've taken the trouble to reach out to them repeatedly are more interested in coming. Easy to do and could pay off.

9. Do a postgame analysis. You've listened to the admission rep, you've watched the presentation, and you've absorbed the video. What now? Take all your notes, write down your impressions, and draw some conclusions about the school; then cross-check your thoughts with website reviews of the college or guidebook descriptions. Sure, website reviews are inconsistent and occasionally slanted, but honestly, so are yours, in the end. Look for common thoughts and similar conclusions, as well as issues of conflict, to help round out your impressions of the school. And if you had a friend, or (gasp) parent, who went with you to the college night, hit him or her up for an opinion: sometimes they might have noticed something you didn't.

10. If you're still interested, follow up. Thank-you notes, further questions, and e-mail pings are, in many cases, quite welcome. Feel free to use the admissions portal available to all students or any direct contact that's provided on the website to continue showing your interest in a school. Especially when you are a potential applicant, many colleges welcome (and log) the contact. Get your questions answered and show your interest in a school simultaneously by following up a school visit or evening presentation by continuing the conversation by e-mail.

EXTRA POINTER. Follow the admission officer's clues about further contact. Some reps love e-mail exchanges and running conversations, others wince when they see an e-mail from a student in their in-box, and still others want phone calls. Luckily, they'll let you know what they prefer before you commit a faux pas. If they don't, feel free to ask, "What's the best way to get answers to questions later on?" They'll tell you what they prefer to do going forward.

Do's and Don'ts for Attending College Fairs

College fairs are the "speed dating" of admissions: you meet a lot of potential partners, have a few minutes to size up the chemistry, then make some snap judgments (many of which need further investigation). So what's the point of a college fair, then? Admissions officers use these mass gatherings to get as much information, both verbal and written, into as many students' hands as possible and to begin their work of building an applicant pool. Students, on the other hand, can use these outreach efforts by admissions professionals to get a glimpse at what a large variety of colleges are about. As in any look-over for a potential relationship, there are some basic rules for getting off on the right foot.

DO get thyself to the fair. Although some of the larger college fairs might seem a little intimidating to students starting the college quest, it's really quite a painless experience. College reps (or sometimes a local alumnus (or alumna) of the college) would like to meet you and see what you have to offer (just as you'd like to meet them and see what they have to offer). There's usually a casual, good-natured atmosphere to be had, if you stop to chat for a few minutes, take a brochure, and get yourself on the mailing list.

IOHO. College fairs are probably the most useful in the fall or winter of your junior year, because that's the jumping-off point for your search. Any earlier and you're likely not to be ready to ask the right questions; any later, and you're beginning to fall behind the pack.

DO dress the part. If your school has a dress code, follow it at the fair. If it doesn't, then just look presentable, that is, polo or collared shirts, khakis or at least semi-dress pants, and so on. You don't need a coat and tie, especially if you'll be pulling on the collar in discomfort the whole time; you don't need a party dress, but don't come straight from the soccer field in your sweaty jersey or look like you are on your way to see the Red Hot Chili Peppers. In general, avoid the extremes.

DON'T bring the folks (or, at least, DON'T walk around with them). College fairs are meant to be student-to-admission rep interactions. Parents, no matter how well meaning, interfere with that valuable time and can be seen by the rep as helicopter parents (hovering uncomfortably over their students) or, worse, lawnmower parents (mowing down everything that gets in their kid's way). If your parents have questions, write them down, ask their questions yourself, and bring a report back to your parents.

DO head right for your first choice(s). Know the "amusement park rule"? Whether it's Six Flags, Disneyland, Knott's Berry Farm, or your local water park, always head right to the most popular ride as soon as the gates open, because the line will grow ridiculously long very quickly. So, too, at college fairs, the best colleges will have long lines to speak to their reps, especially in larger cities or when lots of high schools are invited.

EXTRA POINTER. Some college reps will get lots of attention; others might not talk to a single person. Be respectful of a less popular college and its space. Don't borrow their pen, lean on their table, or block access for students who might want to talk to that college. It's just polite.

DON'T approach only the colleges you've heard about. It's the most natural thing in the world to want to visit only the colleges you've heard of, whether at your school or on ESPN. But the college fair is a very excellent way to expand your horizons and to find relevant alternatives to the few colleges you might already be considering.

Take a chance on a college rep who looks lonely. Many great college matches have been made randomly, so widen your view and give the less popular colleges a shot.

DON'T be a wallflower. A familiar face to any rep at the college fair is the "cruiser": the student who walks up and down the aisles at a quick pace, making it seem like he or she is taking in the passing show but never really stopping to engage any of the college reps. Most often, one would guess, it's simply shyness: this student is not quite sure what to do, not quite sure what to say, not quite sure how to put him- or herself forward to best advantage. Remedy? Realize that the reps are there for you and would actually *like* to meet you, answer your questions, and hear your concerns. Get what you came to get: a sense of the college and how you might fit in there.

DO be prepared with a few questions—especially questions that you wouldn't expect to find answers for on the college website. Try to probe how you would fit in the college (Do you have an out-of-the-way major in mind? Are you interested in working with a professor or getting an internship? Is it important to you to meet students from different backgrounds and from different countries?) Whatever your specific concerns, ask away.

EPIC FAIL! Although admission reps love thoughtful questions, they bristle at awful ones because they make them feel that your curiosity about their college is surface level. Does it really matter if freshmen can have cars? Will you decide whether or not to apply based on the AP policy? Don't come across as indifferent or shallow by asking poor questions.

DO write it all down. Keep a college notebook or folder for business cards, brochures, mailings, and your own notes on what you learned—and the name of the person you met. When it comes time for you to fill out the applications you might be able to use those details (for instance, by referencing in the supplemental questions on the application your discussion with the admissions rep). And trust us—you won't remember.

DO fill out the contact card. Many college representatives will offer you a small card or information sheet to fill out; in every case you should. You might think "the last thing in the world I need is more e-mail cluttering up my in-box or more catalogs jamming my mailbox," but some colleges use the forms you fill out at the fair as expressions of interest in attending their college (some colleges even tabulate how many contacts you've made with their college as a way of gauging how likely it is that you'll come, if accepted, so even if you've already given the college your info, don't hesitate to give it again if asked). Come next fall, you might even get a special application via e-mail called the "fast app" or "snap app" in the trade; for more information on these contacts (which sometimes can mean no more than that the college bought your name from a list), check out:

WWW.PROPUBLICA.ORG/ARTICLE/THE-ADMISSION-ARMS-RACE-SIX-WAYS-COLLEGES-CAN-GAME-THEIR-NUMBERS and

WWW.NYTIMES.COM/2006/07/30/EDUCATION/EDLIFE/INNOVATION.HTML?_R=0.

BONUS DO. Worried you won't have time to fill out all the contact cards or forms? Some college fairs will mail you out a bar code if you register in advance, which the colleges then scan at the fair itself. And, if this isn't offered, you might want to preprint a page or two of labels with your name, address, e-mail, high school, and academic areas of interest, then at the fair all you'll need to do is peel, stick, and move onto the next.

BEST-KEPT SECRET. You might not have thought of this, but after the fair some admissions officials go back to the contact form and fill in their own notes about things that might have struck them about one or other student they met: a sort of instant recommendation.

E-MAIL ETIQUETTE. In the course of your college quest, especially at schools where "demonstrated interest" (that is, your having repeated contact with the admissions staff) counts, you'll have occasion to reach out by e-mail many times. But writing an admissions person, or a college rep, or (in some cases) even a departmental advisor or professor, is a different kettle of fish than texting, tweeting, or snapchatting your best buddy. Here are some things to consider before clicking "Send":

✔ **E-mail is forever.** Once you send it off, you can't get it back. Anything you send to admissions personnel might actually go into your application file—and be there when they're considering whether or not to let you in.

✔ **E-mail goes where it's told.** Check—and double check—to see that the right address appears in the "TO" line. Just because your mom and regional rep are both named Megan is no reason to send "all your love" to an admissions officer.

✔ **Admissions officers might not like–or even open—mail from youwantme@hotbod.com.** Make sure you use an "acceptable" e-mail address, like your.name@gmail.com.

✔ **Subject lines are for subjects.** Put a brief explanation of the nature of the e-mail (like "question about early decision" or "financial aid question") in the subject line. Never include demands such as "Urgent request: immediate response needed" (it's not their fault that you haven't thought to ask 'til the day it's due).

✔ **Salutations matter.** The safest way to start is with "Dear Mr. or Ms. So and So" (using their last name)—or use the title on their business card or the admissions web page. Less good: "Hey, Kate," or "Yo, Joe."

✔ **Clear and concise is best.** Your admissions rep might get twenty-five to thirty e-mails a day. So it's best if you ask your questions in as focused and succinct a way as possible (hint: it's often good to number your questions). And if your question is very elaborate or multifaceted, it's best to call the admissions or financial aid office. You'll get better service that way.

✔ **THIS IS NOT A SHOUTING MATCH.** Don't write in all uppercase letters (which is an e-mail convention for anger or other strong emotion). No one likes being yelled at.

✔ **No one really likes emojis and smileys.** Trust us on this one. ☺ ☻

✔ **This is not Facebook.** Don't write the admissions rep in the same way you'd post on your friend's wall.

✔ **This is not texting.** So pls dun wrte llk ur txtN. uz abbrz @ yor own rsk. coRec me f lm wrng. (Translation thanks to www.TRANSL8IT.COM, which features a neat little Facebook widget.)

✔ **Spelling mistakes make you look like a doofus.** So always use the spel check and proofread yyour email, two. Grammar mistake are not so good, either.

✔ **Sign-offs and signatures count.** Always end by thanking your admissions rep for his or her time and closing with "Best wishes" or "Regards" (or some other relatively formal but friendly closing). And always sign with your (entire) real name, not some wacky nickname like Ry-Ry or Biff.

✔ **Your rep doesn't want to hear your philosophy of life.** Skip the cute quotes or statements of your religious or political views at the bottom of your e-mail. You never know what offends.

The 10 Biggest Financial Aid Mistakes—and How to Avoid Them

You're buying a product than can cost anywhere from three- to seventy-five thousand dollars—a year. The price isn't clearly disclosed at the beginning, and even to get some idea of what you're going to pay, you have to fill out screens and screens of online data, in some cases not even knowing where to put the data. It's college financial aid. And it's a real zoo. Is it any wonder that any mere mortal is utterly confused about the system and often makes mistakes—some of which come back to bite him or her? Luckily, you'll avoid some of the biggest ones—and with any luck save yourself piles of cash—if you look over our 10 biggest financial aid mistakes (and some ways to avoid them).

1. Not understanding the forms. Depending on what schools you're applying to, there are one or two forms to fill out. The basic *FAFSA* form ("Free Application for Federal Student Aid") asks you, and in most cases your parents, to provide relevant financial information, most of it from the 1040 (or 1040A) tax form for the calendar year ending in the middle of your senior year. There are a variety of due dates starting in January of your senior year—check here to see what it is for your state—**HTTPS://FAFSA.ED.GOV/DEADLINES.HTM**—but it's to your advantage to get it in as early as you can after January.

The *CSS/Profile* form is a much more complicated financial inventory, also due in the first few months of your senior year (the exact date is set by each college), used by more than 600 colleges, typically the more selective private colleges. Here, depending on the college, you might be asked more probing questions about the value of your home, how close your parents are to retirement, how much they've contributed to their pension in the last year, whether they own a small business, whether they're married or divorced, whether you have any money in a 529 college savings plan, and so on, and so on.

Keep in mind that if the school asks for the Profile form, they'll also want the FAFSA form, so double the pleasure, double the fun.

 ON THE WEB. All the information is available at HTTPS://FAFSA.ED .GOV/ and HTTP://STUDENT.COLLEGEBOARD.ORG/CSS-FINANCIAL-AID-PROFILE.

 BEST-KEPT SECRET. There are big differences in "methodology", that is, in how colleges calculate your financial aid award, especially among colleges that use the Profile form. For example, different schools calculate need according to different formulas; some colleges cap the equity in your parents' house (if they have one) differently; some include different measures of gift, loan, and your work contribution in their awards; and some expect different contributions from your or your parents' savings (if any). While the net price calculator can give you a ballpark figure about all of this, and while on the financial aid websites of some colleges some information about their methodology is provided, it's a good idea to keep a very open mind about what the final figures will be for you—and how they might differ from college to college.

 ON THE WEB. For a very useful, and detailed, explanation of the different financial aid methodologies (and what they might mean to you), have a look at WWW.FORBES.COM/SITES/TROYONINK/ 2014/11/28/2015-GUIDE-TO-FAFSA-CSS-PROFILE-COLLEGE-FINANCIAL-AID-AND-EXPECTED-FAMILY-CONTRIBUTION-EFC/. Geeks will love it.

 ON THE WEB. One site that might help you with the FAFSA is WWW.COLLEGEGOALSUNDAYUSA.ORG/PAGES/DEFAULT.ASPX.

2. Not setting a budget. Just as with cars and with houses— where the most expensive models can cost ten times as much as the least expensive—it's important that you have some idea of how much you're willing to spend for college. It doesn't have to be too exact—a five to fifteen thousand dollar window can be appropriate, especially because it's hard to determine at the outset what financial aid you might be getting—but you should have some idea of your upper limit. And, if you're willing to take on debt, that is, student loans, to help pay for college, you should carefully think out how much debt you'll be comfortable with. The piper comes piping for repayment when you finish your four or five years at college, and the ten—or now, even twenty—years of debt that follow can be a real life changer.

3. Thinking the sticker price is the price you'll pay. Some students are lucky enough to be able to pay the "rack rate" for college (that is, the full list price) either because their parents make big bucks or their grandparents or other benefactors have been socking away money for the last 18 years. But for more than 60 percent of students, financial aid is the way to go: the list price can be brought down by a half, two-thirds, or, in some cases, even more. Every college has a net price calculator on their website (though they can differ in length and depth from one college to another) that will give you a ballpark figure of what that college is going to cost you— use it for each of the colleges you're considering. Also useful is the FAFSA4caster (cute isn't it?), **HTTPS://FAFSA.ED.GOV/FAFSA/APP/F4CFORM? EXECUTION=E1S1**, which will give you an idea at least about what federal student aid you might qualify for.

⭐**5-STAR TIP.** Keep in mind that the net price calculator typically won't include *merit*-based aid, that is, scholarships you might win at some schools on the basis of academic, artistic, or sports talent (see tip #5, below). So if the college offers money for one of these (some colleges do, some don't), then the price you pay could be even lower.

ON THE WEB. For a very informative and reasonably intelligible pair of articles on how colleges calculate financial aid, see WWW.FORBES.COM/SITES/TROYONINK/2014/02/14/HOW-ASSETS-HURT-COLLEGE-AID-ELIGIBILITY-ON-FAFSA-AND-CSS-PROFILE/ and WWW.FORBES.COM/SITES/TROYONINK/2015/02/28/PAYING-FOR-COLLEGE-HOW-TO-POSITION-ASSETS-TO-QUALIFY-FOR-MORE-COLLEGE-FINANCIAL-AID/.

 BEST-KEPT SECRET. If your family income is less than $65,000—or between $65,000 and $125,000—you might qualify for a full ride, or at least free tuition, at a number of elite schools. Go to WWW.BLOOMBERG.COM/NEWS/ARTICLES/2015-04-01/TEN-ELITE-SCHOOLS-WHERE-MIDDLE-CLASS-KIDS-DON-T-PAY-TUITION to find out what some of these schools are. Then check with the individual colleges to see how they calculate income, and whether any of the forms or schedules on your parents' income tax (for example Form 1040 or Schedule C or E) would disqualify you from getting the free, or greatly reduced, tuition (it's not just your income; there are often a number of conditions).

4. Assuming a state university will be cheaper. We've seen this mistake dozens of times, especially when students are relying on their parents for information. It used to be that not only were the state universities in your home state cheaper than private colleges (because you get in-state tuition) but also state universities in other states (where you have to pay out-of-state tuition) were still cheaper than many private colleges. No more. That's because major state universities now view out-of-state students as "cash cows": as a way of decreasing the state U's dependence on the legislature, they charge out-of-state students as much as a private college would. Upshot? When applying to state universities outside your state, get the facts. And don't think it'll be easy to establish state residency after a year or two; they've got that thought out, too.

BEST-KEPT SECRET. A number of state schools offer in-state tuition to students from other states, especially neighboring ones. Find out if this is true for any state universities you're considering.

5-STAR TIP. A number of private colleges will put together financial aid packages to match the price of tuition and fees at the flagship state university in their state. Always ask.

5. Not knowing the difference between merit-based and need-based aid. You might have thought that if you're a brainiac—top of your class, great SAT/ACTs, boatloads of AP courses, and so on—you'd be a shoo-in for large cash awards at fancy colleges. Guess again. Some of the schools you might want to apply to award aid only on the basis of need—that is, how much help they think you need to be able to afford to go to their college; so no matter how smart you are, you won't be getting scholarship money if your family can afford to foot the bill. However, some schools have money to award on the basis of merit—could be academic, athletic, or artistic—a way of buying talent. In every case, use the financial aid page of the college website to see what aid is being offered.

5-STAR TIP. Of course if one or other of the colleges you're considering offers only need-based aid and your family income or assets are too high to qualify, you'll want to discuss this with your parents (or whoever else is paying). No point applying to a school that your parents aren't prepared to fund even if you get in (we've seen this happen more times than we want to remember).

ON THE WEB. For a list of schools offering the most merit-based aid (by both percentage of students and by average amount) check out WWW.NYTIMES.COM/INTERACTIVE/2012/07/08/EDUCATION/ EDLIFE/8EDLIFE_CHART.HTML. Be sure to click on the headers to sort by percentages and amounts, not just alphabetical names of schools.

Also useful is WWW.KIPLINGER.COM/TOOL/COLLEGE/T014-S001- KIPLINGER-S-BEST-VALUES-IN-PRIVATE-COLLEGES/INDEX.PHP?TABLE=ALL.

6. Not knowing which colleges guarantee to meet 100 percent of demonstrated financial need—and what it means when they don't. Even among schools that award aid on the basis of financial need, not all schools have the resources to provide all the needed aid to all the students they admit. Those that do commit themselves to meet 100 percent of demonstrated financial need. Now not all schools have the same conception of "demonstrated need": some might take into account (some or all of) the equity in your house as a possible resource, some might expect more or less work contribution from you, and, most important, some might include the dreaded loans as part of the package (others might give mostly gift aid, with some small amount of work requirement, especially if the school is well capitalized, that is, has lots of money). Use the net price calculator at each college to see how they might be constructing an offer.

EXTRA POINTER. Be on the lookout for the phrase "loan-free." That means the school will meet whatever percent of demonstrated financial need (100 percent in the best case) without including any loans in the package. Wouldn't it be great to walk away from college without the $30,000 of debt that the average student in this country has?

BEST-KEPT SECRET. Just because some college doesn't guarantee to meet 100 percent of need doesn't mean that they won't, especially if you're a desirable applicant to them, better than they might ordinarily get. If you're a good catch for some school, don't assume you won't get enough aid.

 RULE OF THUMB. If you are in the top 20 percent of the admissions profile, you're likely to get 100 percent of need (though at some especially choosy schools the odds are less).

 ON THE WEB. For a list of colleges that guarantee to meet 100 percent of need, go to any of the following sites:

WWW.USNEWS.COM/EDUCATION/BEST-COLLEGES/PAYING-FOR-COLLEGE/ARTICLES/2013/09/18/COLLEGES-THAT-CLAIM-TO-MEET-FULL-FINANCIAL-NEED-2014

WWW.THECOLLEGESOLUTION.COM/LIST-OF-COLLEGES-THAT-MEET-100-OF-FINANCIAL-NEED/

WWW.COLLEGEXPRESS.COM/LISTS/LIST/COLLEGES-THAT-MEET-THE-FINANCIAL-NEEDS-OF-STUDENTS/349/

Be sure to verify that any colleges you're applying to still meet 100 percent of need, as some colleges might have changed their policy.

7. Not applying to enough schools. If financial aid is an important consideration in your choice of colleges, you should be sure to apply to enough colleges. Financial aid offers can vary widely, even among schools of the same type—a recent comparison we did using the net price calculators of seven schools that we thought would be similarly priced netted prices from $8,000 to $33,000 a year (an astounding range). In order to be safe, apply for more, rather than fewer, schools (ten to fifteen wouldn't be too many). Then, compare what comes out the other end.

EXTRA POINTER. Always apply to the state university system in your home state and the community or city college in your own community. That way, if all else goes wrong, you'll still have a relatively inexpensive place to go to college.

8. Not applying for outside scholarships. Many students think that the college admissions and financial office is the only possible source of funds. But, in truth, college-provided aid can be supplemented by grants from church groups, civic organizations, and even businesses at which your parents work. Your high school college counselor might be getting hundreds of such announcements each year; be sure to check with him or her to see if you qualify for any. Also, most states provide supplemental funding, which in some cases can be quite substantial, through their department of higher education (do a web search for "department of higher education" plus your state name) to see what's available. And if you qualify for National Merit money, be sure to cash in your chips for that, too.

 ON THE WEB. A very comprehensive and useful article on outside funding is at HTTP://ONLINE.WSJ.COM/ARTICLES/HOW-TO-WIN-THE-COLLEGE-SCHOLARSHIP-GAME-1408126980.
        And, for state scholarships, check out
        WWW.SCHOLARSHIPS.COM/FINANCIAL-AID/COLLEGE-SCHOLARSHIPS/
        SCHOLARSHIPS-BY-STATE/.

 BEST-KEPT SECRET. Be sure to check each of your parent's employers to see if any of them have fellowship programs. Sometimes, if your parent is working for a big enough company, they offer college money as an employee benefit.

ON THE WEB. An interesting and unusual list of scholarships can be found at WWW.CBSNEWS.COM/MEDIA/PROSPECTIVE-STUDENT-9-UNIQUE-SCHOLARSHIPS-TO-CONSIDER/.

9. Thinking that if you apply early decision (ED) you can't get aid. It's a common myth that if you apply ED (see "Applying Early? 10 Questions to Ask If You're Considering Early Decision or Early Action" for more on what ED is and how it works) you can't apply for financial aid. The reality is that not only can you apply for financial aid (provided you get the documents in earlier) but also in certain cases you might actually get more money because schools get the entire budget early in the year and have lots of cash available to woo deserving students (this assumes that the school is awarding merit-based aid; if they're doing needs-based aid, you'll get whatever they deem you need, just like regular decision).

 REALITY CHECK. If differences in aid awards make a big difference to you, you'll probably want to apply regular decision to many colleges, compare the awards, and try to get the college you really want to match some of the other awards.

10. Assuming that a parent who isn't living with you is out of the (financial) picture. Fifty percent of American kids have divorced parents; so it's not too surprising that many students applying to college have divorced parents. Now you might have thought that the parent whom you're not living with needn't do anything for you to apply for financial aid. Depends on the college. If you're applying to a state school, which uses only the FAFSA form, then you won't need to enlist the help and financial information of the absentee parent. Only what's called the custodial parent—that is, the one you've lived with most of the year or, if it's a tie, the one who provided most of your support—fills out the form. But, for many private colleges using the CSS/Profile form, the noncustodial parent also has to disclose his or her information on the Noncustodial Parent's Profile (for some colleges, if either biological parent is remarried, you'll have to submit financial information from each of the new spouses). Leave it out and the financial aid office will probably consider the application incomplete.

 ON THE WEB. Useful information about divorce and financial aid can be found at HTTPS://STUDENTAID.ED.GOV/SITES/DEFAULT/FILES/ FAFSA-PARENT.PDF and WWW.FINAID.ORG/QUESTIONS/DIVORCE.PHTML.

 BONUS MISTAKE. Don't rely only on the admissions officer for information about financial aid. Financial aid can be quite complex and the basic information that admissions reps offer at college nights or college fairs might not be exact to your situation. Check out the *financial aid* page of the college website for precise information, but if you can't find the answer to your specific question there, call, e-mail, or visit a financial aid counselor at the college (at some schools, the regular admissions counselors aren't even authorized to talk about financial aid). Ask "how do you calculate financial aid and what might I qualify for" (be sure to have a phone, tablet, or pencil ready to record their answers, especially if they are detailed). Then ask any follow-up questions you might have about the particularities of your financial situation—for example, "does your college put any cap on how they value the equity in our house?" or "does it matter whether my trust fund is in my or my parents' name?" (your parent can participate in the call or visit if the questions are unusually technical, as they often are). A consumer informed is an informed consumer, and it's good to get the information right the first time.

Applying Early? 10 Questions to Ask If You're Considering Early Decision or Early Action

For some students, one of the most perplexing aspects of the college application is whether to apply Early Decision (ED) or Early Action (EA) to the college(s) of their choice. In exchange for a commitment to go to that school—or maybe not—you get the security of finding out whether you got in or not by the end of the first semester of your senior year—and, in some cases, you actually increase your chances of getting in. But how does it all work? And is it right for you? You'll know the answers to these questions if you ask yourself these ten questions.

1. Do I clearly understand the differences among the early application programs—and what each one commits me to? Hey, it's alphabet soup out there: EA, ED, SCEA, and even EN and RD. But, really, the basic distinction is between ED—early decision—and EA—early action. *Early Decision* is binding: in exchange for some bump in your chances of getting in at some colleges, you agree to accept that college's offer (and only that college's offer) if you get in. *Early Action*, by contrast, is nonbinding: even if you are admitted to that college, you're free to accept any other college's offer of admission (and financial aid). And, unless it's the special variety of EA called *Single Choice Early Action* (SCEA)—in which case you generally cannot apply to other colleges' (or some specified set of colleges') EA or ED (one bite per customer)—you usually can apply to as many colleges, EA, as you would like (and are still free to accept any offer of admission and aid you might get). (For careful readers, EN is early notification, while RD is regular decision.)

2. When is it good to apply ED? Early Decision works best either for students who've carefully researched all the relevant options and come up with the one school they really want to go to (no matter where they get in) or for students who have a very special thing they want to study and have found a college that really excels in that. Also, ED works best for students who are really ready to write their final application before the often-earlier-than-usual deadline. If you feel your college application would be stronger if only you got better grades in the first semester of senior year, or took the ACT or SAT another time, or drummed up another, better, letter of recommendation, it'd be prudent to apply regular decision (RD).

3. But is ED right for me? This is a very important question—one only you can answer. You've got to be 100 percent—or at least 99 $\frac{44}{100}$ percent—sure that this college is so special that you're willing to give up all your other chances just to apply to it. And you have to be sure that you know enough about this college to make it your #1, A+ choice. Ask yourself: *Have I not only read up about the college but also visited it? Does it have an absolutely stellar or unique program in what I want to study or are equal opportunities available elsewhere? Would I like the social life and living arrangements or would I be less than fully comfortable in that environment?* Most important, *would I still pick this college if I had handfuls of other opportunities laid out in front of me (perhaps some with better money), or does it just seem good to me now because I don't yet have any other acceptances?* If you're not sure what your answer is to one or more of these questions, the commitment that comes with ED may not be right for you.

4. Does applying ED—or EA—increase my chances of admission? If so, at which schools and by how much? Applying EA usually does not increase your chances of admission, but applying ED can boost your chances at some schools. That's because, like the airlines, some colleges are concerned about "yield management": making sure that they get enough students (and, in some cases enough full-paying students) to fill the upcoming class. So, in exchange for your iron-clad guarantee to attend if admitted, they offer you a somewhat better chance of being admitted. ED will help most at a school at which you are close to admission anyway; applying to the shoot-for-the-moon school is usually a waste of time and a needless depressant when you get summarily rejected.

EXTRA POINTER. If you're not sure whether applying ED will materially help your chances at a particular school, try to ask the admissions rep (preferably privately so they can give a more candid answer) at a college rep visit, college night or fair, or at an information session when you're visiting the college. Pay very close attention to the exact wording of the answer you're given and, if it's unclear to you, ask a follow-up question to clarify. Admissions reps are trained to be quite careful in formulating answers to this question, so they'll choose their words precisely.

RULE OF THUMB. If your SAT or ACT score isn't reasonably close to the top of the 25 to 75 percent band of admits (or better), it's probably not worth applying ED.

EXTRA POINTER. Many colleges have rolling admissions— that is, starting in early fall they accept students as they get applications rather than waiting to a single reply date. Such rolling admissions plans usually do not conflict with either ED or EA, so you can apply both to an ED college and a school that has rolling admissions—thereby maximizing your chances of getting in and of hearing early (of course, if you get in to the ED school you'll have to go there, but that's always the case when you apply ED).

5. Can I apply ED (or EA) if I know I need financial aid? It's a common myth that you can't apply ED or EA if you need aid. In fact, earlier in the year is the time in the year that colleges have their maximum financial resources available (this can be an important factor in your favor at less affluent institutions). Although you won't receive your final financial aid award until you finish the required paperwork—usually in the spring—you can get a tentative aid award as soon as you're admitted. Nevertheless, if you will be needing significant financial aid, there are a number of cases in which you should think twice before applying ED:

▶ if you are seeking merit-based aid but the ED college you're considering offers only need-based aid

▶ if the ED-school you're considering does not guarantee to pay 100 percent of demonstrated financial need but some other equally good school does (however, if you're at the very top of the school's SAT/ACT band of admits, there's a good chance they'll come up with 100 percent)

▶ if you haven't really discussed the costs of your ED school with your parents (or grandparents or other payers) and you're not sure they'd really be able—or willing—to pay if you got in

▶ if you want to be able to compare financial aid offers from many schools and possibly negotiate one off against another (for more on this, see "Top 10 Tips for Assessing the Financial Aid Offer" at the very end of chapter 6)

▶ if after doing the net price calculator at the ED college's website you just can't see how to make this college work financially

▶ if you're just not sure you love that school (and, come to think of it, you might fall in love with some other school if you only investigated it more closely).

IOHO. For most students, in most circumstances, ED is not the way to go.

6. What happens if, after I get into my ED school, my situation changes? Say, my father is laid off, I land a better SAT score, or I get into a better college? Colleges will make allowances if, because of some unexpected economic or family event, you're no longer able to attend the school. No one is going to jail for reneging on an ED commitment if the plant at which your dad has worked for thirty years closes down or if you need surgery and have to meet a $6,000 deductible. But for more garden-variety changes in circumstances— such as all of a sudden you're in a better academic position to get into a better school or even do get into a better school—colleges aren't so accommodating. Some colleges might talk to one another: in the worst case both can rescind their offers of admission (and financial aid). And a few colleges threaten a big cash penalty (say, one semester's worth of tuition) if you back out to go elsewhere. In any case, it's not nice to give your promise, receive some consideration in return, then welch on the deal. Upshot? If, barring some genuine emergency, you're not really planning to go to the school if accepted, apply EA (or SCEA): then you're not at all boxed in.

7. What happens if I get an ED acceptance and the financial aid package isn't enough? Am I still bound? Here, too, common sense prevails. If the ED financial aid offer is far short of what you were expecting—or what it's reasonable to expect given your family's financial situations—many colleges will let you out of your commitment. On the other hand, though, no college is sympathetic to a request for more money so that you can live as a king or queen on their dime. So unless you're reasonably sure you'll be able to afford that college given their likely financial aid offer (see question 5 above for reasons for pause), you'll be better off applying EA or RD.

 ON THE WEB. Check out this interesting article NYTIMES.COM/ 2007/11/04/EDUCATION/EDLIFE/STRATEGY.HTML?_R=0 to see how some admissions officers view backing out of an ED offer.

---

8. What happens if I don't get in to my ED school? Will I still be considered at that same school for regular decision? If you haven't been accepted ED, there are generally two possibilities. If your application is judged competitive with the usual pool of applicants, the college will automatically defer your application: you need to do nothing and your application will be rolled over for regular decision consideration (though it can be a good idea to contact your admissions officer and let them know of your continued interest—keep in mind that some schools track student interest as part of the process). If, however, your application falls far short you'll simply get rejected, in which case, game over (at least at this school). In either case, you go on with your application life: your EA and RD applications now take over.

BEST-KEPT SECRET. At some schools, there's a second round of ED, typically in January or February, called (not too surprisingly) ED II. Apply to it, if you haven't applied to ED I. And if you've been rejected by some college for ED I consider applying to another college for ED II (if ED still interests you); generally, if you've been turned down once for ED, you can't apply for another round of ED at the same school. Of course, as before, make sure you understand what this incarnation of ED commits you to; there can be differences from the first-round ED at some schools.

9. Am I applying ED just to avoid the anxiety of waiting until April? If so, is that bad? The college search is stressful for most every student, so it's natural to be tempted to apply ED just to get the thing over (and to have something to say to friends bragging about their ED or multiple EA admissions). But you shouldn't compromise your ability to make a well-considered, appropriate-to-you decision by future peer pressure, parent pressure, or even your own devil-on-your-shoulder pressure. Instead, apply EA or rolling admissions (or both) so that you can both hear early and have made a good choice—the benefits of both worlds.

10. If I've decided to apply to an ED school, does it make sense to apply to a slew of EA schools as well? Absolutely, especially if your ducks are in order (see questions 2 and 3 above) and the colleges' rules allow it (be on guard for the few SCEA schools). Not only do you greatly increase your chances of getting in but also, if you get into your ED school, you're home free. And if you don't, you still could have plenty of EA schools to choose among.

But there's another reason that adding a lot of EA applications to your ED shot makes sense: as you work your way through the applications the tasks get easier and easier. And, if you've had the foresight to do some thinking about your EA applications over the summer, you'll be getting the bulk of your college applications off before the crush of final exams at the end of the first semester of senior year—and, in all likelihood, you'll produce better applications.

3

GOING ON TOUR

At a certain point you need to take the show on the road and make some tours of college campuses. While you can learn lots from the web, from your high school counselor, and from college nights, fairs, and rep visits, there's just some stuff you can only get by putting boots on the ground and experiencing the colleges in real space and real time. You'll be amazed at how much you learn from these visits and how your perception of some, or all, of the colleges will change—maybe a lot, maybe just a little.

There's no question that, in many cases, these tours require a significant expenditure of both time and money. So you certainly want to make the most of these tours and get as much information as you can during your visit. You also want to be sure to get something more intangible from your visit: a better feel for the place and what it would be like to actually go there. This chapter will help you maximize the benefits of your college visits. In it you will learn:

▶ FAQs for planning your college visits

▶ Top 10 things to see and do on a college visit

▶ 21 must-ask questions on the campus tour (and why you should ask them)

▶ 10 things to look for when visiting a class (or two)

▶ Top 12 tips for nailing an on- (or off-) campus interview

FAQs for Planning Your College Visits: A Beginner's Guide

1. What's the point of making campus visits, anyway? Isn't all the information available on the web? While there are tons of very useful information about colleges on the web, nothing beats a real in-person look-over. It's very hard to get a fully accurate feel for the place just by looking at what the college puts on its website—or by scanning conflicting opinions posted on other sites. When you're at the college in person, you can see real students and real professors—and even get a chance to talk to them face to face. You can see actual classes in action, poke your nose into dorms, see what's really being served in the cafeterias, and find out just how hard it is to park on campus. Plus, there are activities offered at the college—information sessions, campus tours, attending classes, stays in dorms, in-person interviews, consultations with admissions staff, and sometimes even professors and departmental advisors—that simply are not available virtually. So, get ready to make the grand tour—and see what you're buying, in the flesh.

2. When should one think of starting to visit—freshman, sophomore, junior, or senior year? How soon is too soon? How late is too late? Although we know of parents dragging their thirteen-year-olds around college campuses, the best time to undertake college visits is during the junior year—or if that doesn't work for you, the very beginning of your senior year. Generally high school students don't have their minds around college during their freshmen and sophomore years, so visits undertaken at that point could be wastes of time—especially because interests can change dramatically over the course of high school. But by the junior year, most high school students have the college search well underway—having met their high school counselor, taken a standardized test or two, and maybe even formulated a preliminary list of where they'd like to apply—so that would be a good time to integrate college visits into the mix.

5-STAR TIP. If you're planning to apply early decision (see "Applying Early? 10 Questions to Ask If You're Considering Early Decision or Early Action" in chapter 2), then a junior-year visit to the college of your choice is a must.

---

3. What's the best time of year to visit the colleges? Over the summer, during spring break, or whenever you happen to be in the area? Most people plan to visit colleges over the summer. After all, that's when everyone has the most free time to travel, and travel to colleges won't require missing any high school classes—and possibly messing up one's GPA, SAT/ACT testing, or AP prep. Unfortunately, that's also the worst time to visit colleges (unless the college you're interested in has special summer programs—some do). The college scene in the summer is totally different from that during the regular year: much smaller classes, often different faculty (graduate students or non-regular faculty), fewer students, and a sense of laid-back-ness that you probably won't find during the school year—in short, a very distorted picture of what the college is really like. A better idea is to go during your spring break, when at least the regular students and the regular faculty members will be there (be sure that *your* spring break doesn't correspond with *their* spring break—you wouldn't want to arrive at the college only to find that their whole student body is in Cancun). Still, the best is whenever, during term time, you happen to be in the area or happen to be able to get to the area: if you're already there it's free, and if you pick your time, well, at least it's convenient for you.

EXTRA POINTER. Spring break can be at any of three different weeks in March. So if you're planning a tour of many colleges, make sure your itinerary avoids the spring break at each of the schools you want to visit. Check out the academic calendar on each of the college's website before setting your trip in stone.

Another way to find out when spring break is at each of the colleges you're thinking of visiting, sortable by states and by individual colleges, is at WWW.STSTRAVEL.COM/COLLEGE-SPRING-BREAK-DATES. Very useful if you have lots of colleges to search.

BEST-KEPT SECRET. At many schools, spring semester ends as early as the third week in April. So if you're trying to coordinate the college's being in session with your high school's *end* of semester, you're going to have trouble. Better idea? Take the time off during your semester.

5-STAR TIP. Many colleges in the South start classes in August, so if your high school is in the North and hasn't started you could visit colleges in August. On the other hand, if you're in the South, and your high school gets out at the end of May, you could visit colleges in early June without missing school.

EXTRA POINTER. Batch your visits and chart an itinerary. The more colleges you can visit on a single trip, especially if you're driving, the cheaper it will be. Some web sites that can help you plan your college visits include CAMPUSVISIT.COM, CAPPEX.COM, GOSEECAMPUS.COM, and TRIPIT.COM. Some of them have tools that will order your itinerary in the most efficient way and some even provide campus maps.

4. Is it best to visit schools during the beginning, middle, or end of the college-application process? And should one visit every school on one's application list? In the best of all possible worlds, it's good to visit all schools that are serious contenders and to visit them early in the process. This gives you the maximum information before the application process is complete and can help you refine and improve your application choices. But realistically, if you're applying to ten or more colleges, it requires quite a bit of time and, in many cases, money to visit them all.

If you don't have the time, energy, or financial resources to do a full set of visits, consider visiting one of each *type* of school you're applying to (large Midwestern state university, college in your own or a neighboring state, small liberal arts college, church-affiliated college, or whatever): sample the wares rather than tasting them all. And if you know you're only going to able to visit two or three schools, save your tour until the *end* of the application process—when you've gotten your acceptances, financial aid packages (if any), and you know where you really might want to go.

BEST-KEPT SECRET. If you can't swing visiting more than a couple of the actual colleges you're applying to, you can still benefit by visiting a similar school near where you live: every state has its own (series of) state universities and community colleges, and most every residence in the United States is within fifty miles of a small, liberal arts college or large megaversity.

IOHO. If your choice is between visiting a lot of schools really briefly and a smaller number really intensively, choose the smaller number. A two-hour visit to a campus to give it the "once over lightly" is often no better than what can be had on the web. (For what you might do on a full-day college visit, see "Top 10 Things to See and Do on a College Visit" coming up next.)

---

5. Should parents go along on the visits? Yes, if possible. Many schools have activities designed specifically for parents who come to visit. And when parents come along on the campus tours, they can provide additional eyes and ears that can help assess (and record—think of them as scribes) differences and similarities between schools. There's often a lot to take in on these visits and having another person to help you record and debrief after the visit can be enormously helpful. Also, parents are likely to ask questions that you might not dare to ask but actually would be nice to know the answers to (How many classes are taught by TAs? How much do you spend on textbooks?).

But probably the biggest reason for parents to come along is that they are likely to be footing a good portion of the bill for college. So they should have the right to see for themselves what they're buying.

6. How long should you plan to spend at each campus? We think you should plan on putting in a full day at each campus to be sure to have a thorough visit (two days, if you're lucky enough to be staying in a dorm). Sure, it's possible to do the basic admissions activities (the information session and campus tour) in half a day. But it's the extra time you spend hanging around at the school, the nonscripted moments—say, when you get a chance to talk to a student in the dining hall or coffee shop who's majoring in the field you're thinking of majoring in, or when you overhear a bunch of conversations in a student lounge, or when you get to talk to a departmental advisor and/or visit a class or two—that might give you the best insights into what it's like to be a student there and help you differentiate between somewhat similar colleges. Also, a longer visit will give you a better chance to experience the environs around the campus, which is good because it is likely that you will actually get off campus from time to time over your four or five years at the place.

EXTRA POINTER. Some colleges have arranged for discount rates at hotels nearby. Check the college website, under Admissions or Prospective Students, for information.

5-STAR TIP. Amtrak offers a special discount for students making a campus tour. Details are here WWW.AMTRAK.COM/BUY-ONE-GET-ONE-50-OFF-WITH-COLLEGE-CAMPUS-VISIT or here WWW.CAMPUSVISIT.COM/AMTRAK/.

7. What should I do in preparation for my visit? The more preparation you can do before the visit, the more you will get out of the visit. The first thing to do is visit the admissions office website and see what activities they offer visitors and at what times they're offered. In some cases you will be able to—or have to—reserve information sessions, tours and other activities online prior to your visit (try to schedule the information session and campus tour one after the other). Stay-overs at dorms nearly always require reservations—and usually they have to be made a long time in advance because space is very limited. Also, reservations need to be made for on-campus interviews if you're planning to do those (these days, not so many colleges offer these, but it's worth checking it out).

EXTRA POINTER. Always be sure to do a basic look-over of the college website before your trip. That way you'll be able to ask intelligent questions of the tour leader, the admissions official, the financial aid person, or whomever you run into on the college trip—and get useful, otherwise hard-to-get answers! Good also to print out a campus map—that way you'll know where you have to be—and to calendar a schedule—that way you'll know when you have to be there.

5-STAR TIP. If you know what you want to study, it is often possible to set up a meeting with an undergraduate advisor in the exact field you want to study. Go the departmental webpage for the field in question, search for the undergraduate advisor, and e-mail him or her to ask if you could set up a meeting. And, after the meeting, ask if he or she could set you up (either in person or by e-mail) with a student in that major. The combination of a faculty person meeting and a student follow-up can give you a real sense of what that college is about—and how it differs from other colleges you might be considering.

8. Should I visit only my "reach schools"? No. In making your college visits it's important that you visit schools at all levels of likelihood of getting in. It's very tempting to visit only the schools you dream of getting in to; but get real, make sure to visit a representative selection of all the schools you're considering—and that are considering you.

9. Is it ever worth revisiting a school? Absolutely. Especially after you have received acceptances and gotten your choice down to two or three colleges, you can use a revisit to compare the schools directly, one against another, and also to examine more carefully factors that might tip the scales in one direction or another (especially if it's a close call between the choices). Also, you should consider a second look if you think you got a poor impression of a campus based on extraneous factors, such as a sudden monsoon, an encounter with a severely demoralized student, or a knock-down fight with your parents in the car. Another visit might give you a clearer—and more accurate—picture of what the school is like.

Top 10 Things to See and Do on a College Visit

You've just spent the last nine hours on I-80 or three hours delayed at O'Hare. But now you're there, at the big U. Building after building, with little plaques saying what departments are located there and who gave the money for all that research. Where to start? What to do? You'll have the very best campus visit if you make sure to see our top ten destinations on any college visit.

1. The admissions office. Just like in Monopoly, when the game begins by placing your token on "Start," so too every college visit should begin with your visiting the admissions office. There you'll not only find an often annotated map of the campus, with suggestions of sites to visit and things to do, but also you'll typically be offered an "information session"—an hour-long presentation conducted by an admissions officer or in some cases an undergraduate student, designed to acquaint you with the college and, sometimes, its admission procedures (take really good notes if they give any info about what they're looking for in admissions).

 5-STAR TIP. Once you've visited a number of these information sessions, you'll begin to realize that many of them are quite similar. Most colleges will tell you that they

> ▶ read applications *holistically* (that is, that they take the whole application into consideration, no one component is necessary or sufficient for admission);

> ▶ consider applications *contextually* (that is, that you're not at a disadvantage if you go to a no-name high school);

▶ are looking for *passion* (that is, they want to see that you really committed yourself to something and did it for many years in high school);

▶ want you to take the *most rigorous courses you can* (especially Honors, AP, and IB courses, if your school has those).

But what you should be on the lookout for are "differentiators"—things that one college says about themselves that other colleges are *not* saying. Recognizing these features will be very helpful not only in eliminating colleges that don't fit what you're looking for in a school (you might not want 12 required core courses if you'd like to design your own program) but also in tweaking your application to highlight features you have that might fit what the college is looking for (say, they value community service and you've done lots of that). Whatever the case, take careful notes: they'll be very useful later when composing your list and doing the actual applications.

---

2. The campus tour. A staple of all college visits is the tour of the college, usually offered via the admissions office by current students, who are distinguished by their enthusiastic attitude and uncanny ability to talk while walking backward. The tour usually covers the main buildings on campus, the library, a dorm (or, at least, the outside of a dorm), the student center, and a sample classroom or, sometimes, a lab or computer center. And undoubtedly you will be treated to a sampling of college lore and traditions: never walk on the big M as you cross the center of the campus, always squeal like a wild boar when passing the president's house—as well as the chance to ask anything you want to know about the college (within reason) from a real, flesh-and-blood student. (For more on things to ask on a campus tour, see "21 Must-Ask Questions on the Campus Tour (and Why You Should Ask Them)," coming soon.)

EXTRA POINTER. At some campuses, and for students at some stages of the application process, there might be the opportunity to interview with a regional representative or other member of the admissions staff. If this is offered, by all means take him or her up on it. You'll learn more from a one-to-one meeting and, relax, they won't be judging you. At least, not too much. (For more on college interviews, check out the admissions page on the college website. And see the section "Top 12 Tips for for Nailing an On- (or Off-) Campus Interview," later in this chapter.)

3. A class (or two). Many colleges now know they have to show the product they're selling—no, not the dating scene or the food court—but the actual classes. Some colleges offer a list of suggested classes to visit, complete with times, places, the name of the professor, and the course title; but even if there's no such official list, the admissions staff will usually be happy to provide information and suggestions geared to your needs and interests. For more information on what to look for when visiting a class, see "10 Things to Look for When Visiting a Class (or Two)," later in this chapter.

 EXTRA POINTER. In considering which class(es) to visit, consider three factors: the schedule of your visit (some classes only meet on two or three days a week); what field or area you might be interested in (good to compare the same field and, if possible, the same course at different schools so you can compare apples to apples); and the level of the class (it's usually best to include at least one first-year or intro class in your visit—indicated in the course schedule by a low number such as 100 or 1000, but not always the lowest number, which can be reserved for remedial courses). And don't shy away from large lectures: if you're going to a mega university, you might have to take some of those.

BEST-KEPT SECRET. In many cases if you're strolling across the campus and happen on a class that might interest you—especially if it's a large class in a ginormous auditorium—feel free to stop in and sit in the back (no one will notice). Parents are allowed, too. One exception, though, is that in high-security campuses (usually in larger, urban centers) you need special ID to even get into the campus building. In such a case, check with the admissions department, or undergraduate advisor in the relevant department, to see if they can get you in (often best arranged in advance of you visit).

 REALITY CHECK. If you're visiting during the summer, keep in mind that summer school courses can be very different animals than their regular term-time brethren: much smaller size, visiting professors, non-regular faculty and even graduate student teachers, more laid-back students, sometimes even slackers, in short, not necessarily what you'll find come fall of your first year. So don't infer too much from a summer school class.

4. A professor or departmental undergraduate advisor. Some, especially small, teaching-oriented colleges, offer you the opportunity to meet a real live professor, typically someone in the field of study you're interested in pursuing or an undergraduate advisor in a department of interest to you. These meetings give you a chance to learn more about the program in your possible major and to get a sense of what the (nice) professors at the place are like.

Here again the admissions office is the place to go to set up a visit with a professor—usually the departmental advisor, departmental recruitment officer, or a faculty member who works in the area closest to your interests. Or, you might try e-mailing a professor or the departmental undergraduate advisor (contact information is available either on the university directory web page or the individual departmental page) in advance of your visit and see if he or she bites.

Many will—especially if you explain your interest in the university or college and the field or major.

EXTRA POINTER. Keep in mind that you're wasting your meeting if you ask for information easily available on the web. Use this meeting to get specific information not available elsewhere.

5. A campus building of special interest to you. The tours don't cover everything, but you can use the campus map and visit the physics department, or the college's museum of musical instruments, or athletic facilities. Some colleges will not allow you into certain places without a college ID (especially the dorms), but many facilities, especially the academic departments, are accessible to all. In some cases, what you see on this "customized" part of your visit will be the deciding factor in your choice between two in-other-ways-quite-similar colleges.

EXTRA POINTER. If you're a practicing member of a religion, you'll want to visit the church, synagogue, mosque, temple, or campus religious organization that you might attend at college. Denominations, and even houses of worship under a single denomination, vary widely, so it's good to see what you'll be getting if you pick that college.

BEST-KEPT SECRET. As you walk through the campus check out the bulletin boards. Often you can get a really good sense of what the campus culture is like by seeing what upcoming events are. Just keep in mind that at some schools anyone is able to post (while at other schools only registered student organizations can post), so what you are seeing may not be school-sponsored or sanctioned activities.

6. The student center (or student union). At most colleges the student center is the hub of campus activities. Not only will you find there a plethora of entertainment and academic options—ranging from video games, bowling alley, food court, art gallery, movie theater, bookstore, computer lab, game room, and so on—but also a variety of student services—writing center, counseling service, career planning and placement, veterans' affairs, and countless others. Check out whatever you think might be of interest to you.

5-STAR TIP. Most college students are quite friendly to prospective students, so be sure to approach a few students (especially if you're at the food court or snack bar) and ask them a couple of questions about what they like (and don't like quite as much) about the school. People-on-the-street info is often more valuable than canned, tour-guide presentations.

7. The bookstore. Perusing the shelves of books (arranged by class) can give you a window into the level of instruction, the sophistication of the work at home, and the amount expected of students at that college. If you're not sure which are the beginning and which are the advanced courses, ask a worker (often a student): he or she will direct you to what you're looking for and even explain to you the four-letter abbreviations for departments (who would have known that SOAS is South Asian Studies?).

8. The dorms (or fraternities or sororities). Though it's not always possible to gain access to a dorm (especially at security-conscious schools), you might be able to get a peek at a room during a campus tour, or—if you're really lucky and really nice—coax a student you meet into showing you his or her room. It's important. We recently visited a college whose name you would know whose dorms weren't air-conditioned (it was eighty-five-degrees the day we visited), which looked like they were built in 1952, and where the curtains looked like they hadn't been cleaned since then. Amazing! Consider the fact that you're going to have to live in one of these places for at least a year (for many students, more). Who can learn well when living in a pigpen?

5-STAR TIP. If the college you're visiting has a stay in the dorm, see-what-it's-like, type of program (check the admissions website), by all means sign up, especially if it's one of the colleges you're seriously considering attending. Nothing beats first-hand experience.

EXTRA POINTER. If someone who graduated your high school a year or two ago is a student at the college you're visiting, consider asking him or her to put you up for a night. Often graduates of your high school are proud of their colleges and will be happy to show you the inside story.

9. The food service. You gotta eat. Check out the choices at the dorm cafeteria, especially if you have any special preferences such as vegetarian, vegan, kosher, halal, gluten-free, or whatever. And find out if there's a choice of dorms in which you can eat: at some colleges you can take lunch, for example, near your classes, and at some colleges different dorms offer different menus.

EXTRA POINTER. Find out how many meals a week you get with your plan: what happens on Saturday and Sunday? And, if you're planning to stay on campus over holidays (e.g., Thanksgiving) and breaks (e.g., winter or spring break), what happens with the grub then? All, good things to know.

10. The town or city. Chances are you'll actually be getting off campus from time to time and it's useful to see how pleasant (or not) the town is and what amenities are offered there. So, if yours is a longer visit, set aside some time for a bit of a walk or drive around town and for stops at places that are important for your lifestyle—whether it's the Thai restaurant, a jazz club, place of worship, art museum, concert hall, the barber shop, or the mall. Life is more than just the college quad—investigate beyond.

 BONUS TIP. Before visiting any campus, you should make a schedule: a list of each of the activities you're going to do (information session, campus tour, sample class, meeting with advisor or professor, lunch at student center)—complete with place and time. Then stick to it, even if some activity doesn't go according to plan or some class or meeting sours you on the school. Sometimes things (and your impressions of them) turn around completely, and if you bail out of the schedule in the middle, you might miss something that would have totally changed your mind. And, to the extent possible, it's good to standardize your activities across the different colleges you'll be visiting. That way you'll be able to directly compare one college against another.

21 Must-Ask Questions on the Campus Tour (and Why You Should Ask Them)

In addition to a general walk-around, the campus tour is your chance to have your questions about the school addressed by a real-live student at the school. This is a great opportunity you should definitely make the most of. Keep in mind, though, that the student leading the tour has likely been selected for his or her upbeat, enthusiastic, and frequently, perky attitude. So the tour guides are always going to put the college in the best possible light and their canned presentation (in many cases) is going to make the school sound better than heaven on earth. However, the guides are always eager to answer questions. So, if you ask the right kinds of questions, in the right way, you can get beyond the sales pitch to an authentic look at what it's really like going to that school. Which is the reason that you're on the tour in the first place. So get ready to fire these queries as you tour the college and be alert to the insights you can gain from the answers you get (and from reading between the lines of the answers you get).

   1. Are the professors good? Who was your best professor? Why? The main thing you're buying at college is an education, so it's important to get some sense of how good the teachers are. The tour guide is likely to assure you that every teacher on campus is awesome, so if he or she is hesitant in answering this question, consider that to be a red flag about the quality of teaching. Also, note what the tour guide thinks was good about their best professor. Admiring a professor just because he or she is charismatic, or clowns around a lot in class, or is a good showman could be a sign that serious learning isn't a big value at the school. However, if the tour guide highlights the professor's knowledge of the field or concern that the students learn, this can be a good sign.

   2. Are the courses challenging? Everyone wants to know how hard the classes are going to be: some students worry about being blown away by killer courses while others hope for courses that will not bore them to tears by being even easier than their high school classes. Asking the question in an open-ended way ("How hard are the courses here?" or "Are there a lot of easy courses here?") will encourage the tour guide to give an objective read on the courses rather than just telling you what they think you want to hear.

3. Are there lots of large lecture classes in the first year? If so, how large? Large lecture classes (i.e., ones bigger than fifty) are not necessarily bad classes, but in general, the quality of learning (and degree of individual attention) is better in smaller-sized classes. It's useful to find out how many large classes you're likely to take—and just how big the largest classes can run—because there's a big difference between having to take one class of 250 students and four classes each averaging 700 students.

4. How hard is it to get into classes? The course offerings in the catalog can look pretty impressive until you realize that there's a two-year waiting list to get into the most popular—and, in some cases, required—courses. The trend in colleges these days (especially at many cash-strapped state universities) is to increase student body without increasing the number of faculty, so it's becoming harder and harder to get into classes at many campuses. Watch out for any long, pregnant pauses or major hemming and hawing as your tour guide addresses this question.

5. How many of your classes have been taught by TAs? Teaching assistants (that is, graduate students as opposed to real professors) are controversial, though indispensable, parts of the instructional staff at many universities. These are teachers-in-training and their quality can vary greatly depending on how good the graduate programs are at that particular school and also, how much graduate work is required before the TAs can teach their own courses. You should assess schools where TAs carry a large portion of the teaching load in this light.

6. Are some of the courses taught online? Are some of the *required* courses taught online? Look, we're not saying that going to college online is necessarily bad. After all, there could be teachers who give a good show online, and there are students who like the ability to take classes when they want and to play back sections of the lecture they haven't fully understood. But some students can't learn this way and much prefer classes with flesh-and-blood professors. Colleges, we think, should disclose—openly and without apology—when you're going to get a less-than-in-person instructor, especially in a required first-year class such as math or English comp. Which is why you should ask.

7. How serious are the students here about academics? You'll want to know whether students are likely to spend their time 24/7 studying or 24/7 partying. Then you can match up your own goals with what the school's culture is.

8. What are the most popular majors here and what majors is the school particularly strong in? This question will help you gauge whether students here tend to be interested in business, science, liberal arts, or whatever. Also, it's good to know if the school is particularly strong in particular fields: if your interests lie in one of these areas, picking that school and doing that major may offer some real advantages in your life post-college. And, while you're at it, you might want to ask if everyone can get into a major: some majors, especially arts ones, require auditions, portfolios, or other materials in order to be accepted. Important to know.

9. What are the requirements like and how easy is it to place out of them? Surely you don't want to show up at your new college only to learn for the first time that everyone at the place is required to take four lab sciences, or three years of foreign language, or write a hundred-page senior thesis? Or that you'll have to take exactly the same Spanish or American History course you took in high school just because the college (or state legislature) requires it of all incoming students. Ask the tour leader how burdensome were the requirements, and whether he or she was required to take any do-overs or could easily place out (say, by using AP credit or by taking more advanced courses in the same field).

10. Are there lots of opportunities for internships or for collaborations with a professor? Many students report that individual work with professors is *the* most valuable educational experience they had in college, so find out if you could have this opportunity here (especially good is if there are established setups for internships). Ask the tour guide if he or she ever did one-on-one work with a prof and if the work was a substantial research partnership or more like cleaning test tubes or proofreading the professor's papers.

11. Do lots of students go to study abroad? Study abroad is another opportunity that you might like to take advantage of in your later years in college (especially if you want to major in a foreign language or some form of international study). So check to see if this is something that is regularly offered at this college. It's good also to ask if your financial aid goes with you when you study abroad and/or whether there are specific scholarships for study abroad.
Many colleges have substantial moneys set aside to encourage study abroad.

12. Do you ever feel lost at such a big school (or smothered at such a small school)? At college, size really does matter. You probably will know before your visit how large or small the school is (information easily obtained from the school website). But what you might not know is what it's really like to go to a school one hundred times larger than your high school (or 1/10th its size). Ask the tour guide about his or her personal experience and feelings.

13. Do a lot of students live in the dorms and what's the food like? Hey, everybody's got to eat and sleep, so why not figure out what the best dorms are and which has the best food service. Also be sure to find out if most students live in dorms, in off-campus apartments, or commute from home. Having a living arrangement that's vastly different from what most students are doing can put you out of the mainstream and lead to feelings of isolation and alienation.

14. Is there Wi-Fi in the dorms and are the dorms air-conditioned? How're you gonna Facebook, Tweet, Tinder, or Instagram 24/7 if your college is still in the Stone Age? And do you really want to live in a dorm that's hotter than you-know-where?

15. Are fraternities and sororities big deals on campus? Whether you're in a frenzy to go Greek or wouldn't be caught dead at a kegger, this question will let you know how well your attitudes fit in with the rest of the campus. You wouldn't want to pick a school where everyone who counts is living at Rho Rho Rho, while you're slumming it at Zardoz Hall.

16. Where do students like to hang out? What goes on here on weekends? If you're planning on having a life outside classes, you'll want to know what students around the place do in their spare time. Keep the question general (rather than asking about some super-specific interest of yours) so that you can find out what things most students like to do—and what facilities are offered to do them.

17. What's the social life like on campus? How easy is it to meet other students? Are they mostly like you or different? Your tour guide should be glowing about the social scene on campus. If not, take note. The question of whether the students are generally similar to, or different from, your tour guide is an important barometer of the diversity of the student body. It's quite a different experience to be at a school that is more homogeneous—where you could wind up in the minority—and one where there's no one predominant type of student—in which you're free to move in whatever social group you'd like.

18. Do you ever get into the town? What do you do there? Campuses can be pretty fun places, but at many, especially smaller, campuses, students want to migrate into the town or city. The question of whether the environs of the college offer lots of things to do or whether they roll up the sidewalks at 9 pm can have a real impact on your enjoyment at college. Also, in some cases it would be worth it to ask how safe the environs are. You wouldn't want to find out the hard way.

19. If you could change one thing about the school, what would it be? This question could force your guide down from his or her perpetually cheerful guise into an honest assessment of some things that are wrong at the school. However, if your guide is trained enough to turn every negative into a positive ("the only thing wrong about this college is that it's over in four years"), you won't get much useful information out of this question.

20. What's been your best experience at college? Your worst? Here's another way to try to get at the strengths and weaknesses of the school in question—and whether what's cited as strengths or weaknesses would be important to you. If your guide considers something to be a strength that you consider a weakness—well, that's a fact, too.

21. If you had to do it again, would you consider another college? Which one(s)? Probably your guide will not admit (even in a moment of great weakness) that he or she should have gone to a different school given how glorious and wondrous this college is (as you have just seen on the tour). But you might pry out of the tour guide some relevant alternatives that other students consider and that you could consider applying to.

BONUS TIP. Any of these 21 questions can be asked at the information session, if for whatever reason you're not going on the tour. You probably won't get as candid answers if the session is being led by an admissions professional.

10 Things to Look for When Visiting a Class (or Two)

We are big believers that sitting in on a couple of classes is really important to do during your college visit. But it can be puzzling to know what to *do* while you're in that class. Just how are you supposed to assess a class in a subject you might not be all that up on or a class taking place in the middle of a semester? You'll have good success in forming an opinion of how good a professor you're watching—and, by extension, how good the classes are at the college you're visiting—if you ask yourself the following questions as the minutes in the lecture tick by.

1. Does the professor present the material clearly or is he or she in a complete fog? Even though you might be walking into a class in the middle of a semester or even in the middle of a lecture, things shouldn't be a total muddle—especially if you're attending a first-year class that's supposed to be the introduction to a subject. Being able to get the material out clearly, in a way that the students can understand, is a fundamental skill that every professor should have, so if the class makes absolutely no sense—well, that's a red flag.

 5-STAR TIP. Pay special attention when the prof is explaining any technical term or language special to the field. How he or she explains the nonordinary items will shed light on how well he or she can explain the ordinary ones.

EXTRA POINTER. When selecting which class to sit in on, try to pick first-year classes or classes in a field just a step up from your current high school class level. Many colleges will provide you with a list of the most popular first-year classes and these are good ones to select from. It's not reasonable to expect to be able to understand a Calculus 4 class, when you've never taken Calculus 1.

2. Is the professor organized or totally scattered? A good class presents topics in a logical manner rather than flitting from topic to topic for no evident reason. Keep in mind that a class that lacks any discernible structure or order is one that will be very hard to learn in. Think of how hard it would be to study for a test on material presented in what seems to be a random way.

EXTRA POINTER. Look for an outline, PowerPoint, or at least a clear division of the class into sections (preferably with an introduction at the beginning and a summary at the end). Professors who take the time to put up such "signposts" are often professors who've thought the material out carefully.

3. Does the professor seem to know his or her stuff, or does he or she seem unsure about the material? A confident presentation often reflects the professor's mastery of the material and the fact that he or she has taught the course before (and worked out all the kinks). On the other hand, a halting, tentative presentation can reflect the professor's less-than-stellar command of the material—never a good thing.

4. Does the class have at least some entertainment value, or is it deadly boring? Face it, college isn't meant to be "Comedy Central" and most professors aren't going to put on an extravaganza complete with drum rolls and fireworks. (In fact, you should be suspicious if you encounter a professor whose class consists entirely of clowning around because how much are you going to learn from that?) Still, in college you're going to have to sit through hundreds of hour- to hour-and-a-half long lectures, so you surely don't want to be stuck at a school whose classes are 100 percent tedium.

5. Does the professor just lecture or does he or she incorporate some visuals or multimedia? Nowadays most classrooms are set up to project PowerPoint, connect to the Internet, and use a variety of interactive tools (including, sometimes, clickers to poll student response). Look for some of these additional elements to see just how up-to-date the professors and classrooms at this college are.

6. Does the professor seem concerned that students learn or does he or she just want to get through his or her notes? The real job of the professor isn't to just spew out content but rather to ensure that the students learn, so look for signs that the professor in some way or other involves the students. One good sign is if the professor engages the class in discussion or, at least, has breaks in the lecture when the students can ask questions. Less good is when the professor pays only lip service to student questions—trying to get through them as quickly as possible or, worse, totally ignoring hands waving in the audience. Often you can gauge how seriously a school takes teaching by how seriously the professor takes the students in the room.

EPIC FAIL! If the professor comes off as condescending, stuck up, or arrogant, those are other signs that the professor doesn't hold the students in high regard—and probably isn't all that good of a teacher. It could just be a bad egg, but it could also be a sign that good teaching isn't all that important at that school.

7. Does the professor fill the class time or does he or she end early or late? You might not think that watching the clock would net you any useful information, but actually it does. Ending a class early is often a sign of an inexperienced teacher who does not know the material in enough depth to fill the entire period. Going over time can indicate an inexperienced teacher who doesn't know how much material can appropriately be covered in a single class (or it could reveal an experienced teacher who has no regard for the fact that he or she might be making students late to their next class—also not a good thing).

8. Is the course taught at the appropriate level or is it much too easy or hard? If you show up at a college chemistry class and they're explaining what the periodic table is—this is cause for concern. You'll be wasting time and money if you go to a college where all the classes are covering stuff you already learned. However, if you attend a required first-year class and they're using stoichiometry to calculate the molarity of HCl, you might want to give some thought (in certain cases) about whether this school (or at least this class) isn't too challenging for you (see if they have tiered classes for that subject—good if they do).

9. Do the students look interested or are they bummed out? Teaching is a two-way street. So, don't neglect to gauge the reactions of other people sitting in on this class, specifically, the students actually enrolled and taking it. Do they look like they are engaged by the class presentation? Some positive signs: they ask questions, they're assiduously taking notes, they respond to jokes the professor makes, they seem relaxed. Bad signs: they're putting their heads down on the desk and sleeping, they're using their laptops to put in bids on eBay or their phones to text, they are wearing earphones and not actually listening to the professor, or they trickle in fifteen minutes late or migrate out halfway through the class.

EXTRA POINTER. Pay special attention to students sitting at the back of the room. These are usually the most alienated students, even in a good class, so don't think too badly of the professor if there are no signs of life back there. But if you can sense some excitement even in the back rows—now that's a sign of something special.

10. Does the professor seem like one you'd like to learn from? While you're sitting in that class, perform the following thought experiment: Next year (if I go to this school) I might be taking this class or a class very much like it. Would I enjoy learning from this professor and others, perhaps, just like him or her? If the answer is yes, then you've found a college that should be on your "seriously consider" list. If not, well, that's a fact, too.

 REALITY CHECK. Keep in mind that in visiting a single class or two, you're *sampling* the instruction at that school. And, as with any small sample, the results can be skewed.

Top 12 Tips for Nailing an On- (or Off-) Campus Interview

One of the most important—and least-thought-out—parts of the college- application process is the interview. The interview could be on campus with an admissions officer, in your own town or city with an alumnus or alumna of the school, or even by Skype with someone who is at, or who went to, the school. But whoever the question-asker, it's your chance to strut your stuff. And to find out a little more about the school you're considering. You'll up your chances of winning the interviewer over, if you follow our dozen best tips.

1. Step up to bat. Though some schools pitch the interview as "optional," it is almost always worthwhile to take advantage of the chance. Colleges have literally thousands of applicants, so anything you can do to up your chances can only help. It's generally better to help the admissions staff put a personality on the application, and the report the interviewer will write can help them do this—no matter how optional they say it is.

 RULE OF THUMB. The smaller the school, the more importance they put on the interview. Sometimes, if you don't bother to interview they'll even think you don't want to go to their college and throw your application into the "deny" pile (or at least view it less favorably).

2. Pick an on-campus interview. Colleges know that not every student can visit their campus, so they offer remote alternatives such as the Skype interview or the coffee-shop-in-your-home-city interview.

But, if everything is perfectly equal, avoid these choices (if everything is not perfectly equal, these choices will work, too).

REALITY CHECK. Book early—especially if you're wanting to interview in the summer. On-campus interview spaces fill up quickly, so request them as soon as you have any idea that you'll be applying to that college (you can always cancel—no charge). But keep in mind that many schools offer on-campus interviews only during certain months—and not necessarily the month you'll be visiting. Check the admissions page on the college website for exact details.

5-STAR TIP. Some schools only offer interviews to certain students and only at certain times at the admissions cycle (for example, only after you've applied or only after you've made some initial cut). Other schools require *you* to set up the interview (again, in some cases, only after you've applied). Whatever the case, make sure you understand exactly what's being asked interview-wise at each of the schools you're applying to. The admissions page on the college website will tell you what you need to be on top of.

3. Pick a time that's comfortable for you (if you can). You might have thought that bright and early in the morning would be best. Not for all. If you're a morning person, ready to shine at the crack of dawn, that's great. But if it takes you half the day to get in gear and be your best self, aim for an afternoon time. You'll do better if you feel better.

EXTRA POINTER. One advantage of the later afternoon on-campus interview is that it typically takes place after you've had the tour of the campus—thus giving you a chance to think up a few questions that will communicate your interest in going to that college. If you pick a morning time, take the time to prepare a few questions from the college website—perhaps about the character and traditions of the school, the kinds of majors and special programs they offer, or even the clubs and teams at that school.

4. Outfit yourself with the right duds. Every school has a culture that is reflected in how people dress there. Dress appropriately for that campus. Some schools expect that interviewees will wear business-like attire (button-down shirt and nice pants for guys, dress pants, skirt, or dress for gals); others are more casual and easy-going (just about any clean pants or even a polo shirt will do). In any case, pick clothes that fit well and in which you will feel comfortable (brand-new clothes, never worn, are usually not the best choice); you won't want to be tugging at the collar or adjusting your pants throughout the interview.

5. Come on time—and alone. No interviewer likes a student who saunters in 20 minutes late, offering some dumb excuse about why they couldn't find the building or were held up at lunch. Nor do interviewers want to interview your parents (though some might entertain brief questions from your parents after your interview is done). So, unless directed otherwise, leave your parents in the waiting room (or send them off for coffee) while you're visiting with the interviewer.

5-STAR TIP. You'll increase your chances of making it to the interview on time if you check out Google Maps or the college website well before your appointment. And keep in mind that, depending on the school, the interview location might not be at the admissions office or welcome site, so be sure to know exactly where you're going. Also, if you're coming by car, make sure you have some idea where you're going to park. Not every college offers on-campus parking.

EXTRA POINTER. There's no point arriving ultra-early, because the interviewer probably won't see you early, and you'll just sit there waiting, stewing in your own juices.

6. Be prepared with the basics. Make sure you have prepared answers for each of the schools you're interviewing at to the magic three questions: *Why do you want to come to our college? What do you want to study at our college?* (the more particular the better), and *What work have you done in that area?* You're practically guaranteed to be asked these questions and in many cases the success of the interview depends on how well—and with how many detail and specificity—you can answer them.

BEST-KEPT SECRET. A number of colleges say on their website what questions will be asked on the interview or at least what areas will be probed. Be sure to consult this important resource and prepare accordingly.

5-STAR TIP. It might occur to you to prepare a résumé or tear sheet to give to the interviewer. Some colleges welcome this, while others do not allow it. Again, check the website for details.

7. Tailor your answers to the situation. You'll want to make your answers appropriate to the nature of the interview. If you're talking to an admissions officer behind his or her desk, asking you a scripted set of questions, you'll want to answer, simply and directly, just what's being asked (the interviewer might even be noting down how—and how well—you're answering the specific things the college wants to know about you). If, on the other hand, you're having a walk in the park or a trip to the ice cream store with an alumnus or alumna of the school, you'll want to make your answers more conversational and informal. Adjust your answers to the setting. And be sure to let the discussion develop naturally. After all, even an interview is a two-way exchange of information, and you should be sensitive to how the discussion is progressing and what the other person is saying.

5-STAR TIP. Try to keep your answers to a good length. Monosyllabic answers—*bad* (no one wants to talk to someone who has barely anything to say). Droning on and on—*not such a hot idea* (no one wants to be lectured). Keep in mind that the interviewer can always ask a follow-up if he or she is interested in learning more.

BEST-KEPT SECRET. One thing that can help an interview—and help put a human face on you as a candidate—is to have prepared a few tidy stories or anecdotes to liven up the discussion. Of course, the prepared stories have to fit into the ongoing discussion and have to seem authentic, not canned; still, many students can benefit by having prepared a few anecdotes in advance.

EXTRA POINTER. Don't get flummoxed if the interviewer offers no response to your answers. Certain admissions officers or alumni think their job is to just ask a series of standardized questions. and their not commenting on your answers doesn't reflect any judgment on their part.

8. Be aware that there isn't always a right answer. Some questions are thought questions—designed to see how good you are at thinking on your feet and to get some sense of you as a person. Be on the lookout for these questions, where all you need to do is be yourself and try not to sweat them (even if you're used to yes-no questions).

EXTRA POINTER. Many students report difficulty with "least" and "most" questions, for example, "What subject in high school did you like least?" or "What was the most important, nonacademic experience you've ever had?" If you get one of these, don't tie yourself up in knots, weighing one choice against another; just pick one and start talking about it. What's most important is how you develop your thoughts about the question asked, not what particular thing you rank as "most" (or "least").

9. Learn how to finesse difficult questions. Once in a while, you get asked about controversial issues at that particular college. For example, suppose you're asked, "Do you think it would be a good idea for us to disband our athletic program and use the money saved for more academic purposes?" or "Do you think all students in the dorms should be given an opposite-sex roommate?" Don't feel you have to come down 100 percent on one side of the issue—sometimes it's good to recognize and explore both sides of an issue (that way, you come off as thoughtful and nondogmatic). Consider drawing a distinction or staking out a middle ground (for example, if the football team gets into the BCS ranking, some additional funds could be donated to the college; or, different-sex roommates should be given the option of sharing a room, if both agree).

5-STAR TIP. If at all possible, don't go political/religious/lifestyle. Try not to open up hot-button issues by asking questions or making unsolicited statements about religion, politics, sex, and drugs. You don't know what your interviewer's biases are, so why stick out your neck if you don't have to? And, if you're specifically asked about some controversial item in the news, try not to stake out the most extreme position.

REALITY CHECK. Avoid excuses or confessions. No interviewer wants to hear your explanations about why you have a low GPA or why you did badly on the SAT or ACT. (If directly asked, give as short, though honest, an answer as possible). And don't bring up your personal problems. The college interview is an attempt to size up how you'll fit in at their college, not a therapy session in which you get to vent all your difficulties in life.

10. Be authentic. Don't overstate your achievements but, at the same time, don't be too shy to highlight what you've really accomplished. Keep in mind that you're trying to convince the college to admit you, and how will they be able to do that if you don't see what's good about you? However, there's selling and then there's overselling. You want to come off as believable, sincere, and honest—not as a used car salesman.

11. Realize that you're interviewing them, too. Even in the most formal interview there's always room for discussion and for you to ask questions. The half-hour or hour you spend with the college representative is not only their chance to find out about and evaluate you but also your time to find out about them. Keep in mind that someone (you or your parents, grandparents, or the student-loan company) is going to be spending a lot of money for you to go this college, so you're entitled to find out what you want to know from the living, breathing representative of that college.

5-STAR TIP. If you're being interviewed by an alum, ask them about their experience, how they've seen the college change, what their favorite memory was, and how their college experience led (or didn't) to their current career. People love to talk about their memories and about places that meant something to them, and, if the person is interviewing for the college, he or she probably had a great time there.

12. Be friendly. On a bad day, the on-campus interviewer might have to conduct six, eight, or even ten interviews, and he or she is likely to remember the students who were actually nice. Be sure to thank the interviewer at the end for taking the time to talk to you, and say how much you've enjoyed visiting the campus and that you hope to be there in the future. And always send a follow-up, thank-you e-mail, or, even perhaps a handwritten note. Thank-you's are now a standard part of the application etiquette.

4 TAKING THE TESTS

And now the fun really begins. Whether you like it or not (and most likely you won't), standardized tests play a big role in the college-application process. Your scores on the SAT or ACT can make a major difference for your success at gaining admissions to certain schools, maybe even some of the schools you really would like to go to.

Don't adopt the mind-set that there's nothing you can do to affect how well you're going to do on these tests. And don't just throw up your hands and peg yourself as someone who "just doesn't do well on standardized tests"—or, conversely, as someone who "automatically does well on standardized tests and hence need not bother to prepare." These tests have their own peculiarities and ins and outs, so it's important to know what to expect and how to prepare for what you'll be asked to do. That's why this chapter leaves no stone unturned. Here you will find tips—written by someone who himself just went through the process of taking some of these (and got triple 800s on the SAT). You'll learn:

▶ FAQs about standardized tests

▶ How to prepare for the SAT and ACT

▶ Top 10 SAT/ACT test-taking tips

▶ Top 10 tips for the English section

▶ Top 10 ways to make yourself a mathmagician

▶ 7 things you need to know about your calculator

▶ Top 10 strategies for the reading section

▶ The science of taking the science section on the ACT

And if that wasn't enough,

▶ 10 best tips for writing the SAT/ACT essay

FLASH! The SAT will change significantly in March 2016. In this chapter, we'll provide specific tips for both the old (we'll call it "pre-2016") SAT and the new ("2016") SAT. There'll also be general tips that will help you on all standardized tests (pre-2016 SAT, 2016 SAT, and ACT).

For detailed info about the 2016 SAT, see the last section of this chapter "Flash! Big 7 Changes to the 2016 SAT—and What to Do about Them."

FAQs about Standardized Tests

Colleges consider the high school transcript the most important component of an application, but for most institutions an applicant's standardized testing follows close behind. Taking the SAT or ACT can be daunting for a first-time test taker because it requires both basic attention to tasks and more complex testing strategies, so we've provided the answers to a baker's dozen of FAQs to help you stay on top of your standardized testing.

1. Should I take the SAT or the ACT? All colleges will accept either the ACT or the SAT, so you should determine which test fits you best. Historically, the SAT has been more skills-based, which means it evaluates overall test-taking and problem-solving abilities, while the ACT tends to be more course content- and context-based, which means it more often reflects the skills used in the classroom. Both are valid; they just have a different feel to them. It's like Coke and Pepsi—two different corporations, both producing virtually the same product, but some people have a distinct preference for one over the other.

 FLASH! A revised SAT appears in 2016, with the stated goal of the revision being to align the test better with classroom-based skills and material. Some educators have suggested that these changes will make it even more like the ACT, so choosing which test to take will likely become more of a personal preference based on testing schedule or area of the country.

EXTRA POINTER. Not sure which test to take? Try both and examine both your visceral reaction to each test as well as your results. If one feels less pressure-filled or you score relatively higher on one than the other, choose that test. Colleges will accept either and they value both equally. But some scholarships require one or the other; so if you have a particular scholarship in view, enter its requirements into the equation.

2. Do I absolutely have to take standardized tests to go to college? Not always. More than 800 four-year institutions have test-optional or test-flexible polices, with the latter schools giving you the option of submitting standardized testing in different combinations. If your academic performance outpaces your test-taking abilities, strongly consider adding test-optional schools to your college list to improve your range of options.

 ON THE WEB. For a list of schools that don't require standardized tests, check out HTTP://FAIRTEST.ORG/UNIVERSITY/OPTIONAL.

3. When should I take the SAT or ACT? Students often feel pressure to take the SAT or ACT in the fall of their junior year, but what's the hurry? Most students are better off waiting until the winter or spring of their junior year, because they will be older, they will have covered more course material in school, and they are likely to do better, potentially removing months of stress. In the end, you won't score any higher by taking the ACT or SAT earlier in your high school tenure, but you certainly could stress yourself out more.

RULE OF THUMB. A smart baseline plan is to take the SAT or ACT in the winter of your junior year, then again in the spring. At that point you can assess where you might need to prepare or review and decide about your testing plan for the fall accordingly.

 BEST-KEPT SECRET. The standardized tests are offered six or seven times a year, and you don't have to take them in your school or with your class. Pick times when you're most relaxed—not the month you have to take four AP tests—and a location that's convenient for you. Both the ACT and SAT are offered in June (an excellent choice if your school is over by then). If you need a special administration (say, you observe the Sabbath on a Saturday), bear in mind that not every test day qualifies for special administration; also, for some strange reason, one administration of the ACT does not include New York.

 ON THE WEB. You can find upcoming SAT dates and register for the test at HTTPS://SAT.COLLEGEBOARD.ORG/REGISTER/. For the ACT, the comparable site is WWW.ACTSTUDENT.ORG/REGIST/. Make sure the dates you're looking at are for this year (it's easy to get confused).

 REALITY CHECK. Do you have a sense of your testing schedule? If so, sign up as early as possible to get the test location you want. Each test site has a limit to the total test takers they can handle, so if you wait to register, you may find yourself locked out of an easy-to-find, local place and wind up driving to an unfamiliar site, which can be anxiety-provoking on the test day.

4. How do I sign up to take the SAT or ACT? Test registration is entirely online. You will be asked to add some personal and academic information to your registration profile before finalizing your test dates, but it's quite straightforward (have a credit card ready, yours or your parents', because you have to pay up-front).

When you sign up for the ACT (or the 2016 SAT), you have the option to take it with or without the writing (essay) component. Some colleges require the writing section so if you're thinking that you might even possibly want to apply to one of those, be sure to sign on for the test with writing. Err on the side of caution: as you move forward in the college-application process, new colleges might pop up, some of which want to see the writing sample. If, however, you're 100 percent sure that you're certifiably a terrible writer, you will want to bypass the writing section and adjust your application list accordingly. (Note that for the pre-2016 SAT, the essay component is automatically included.)

 REALITY CHECK. Check the admissions page of each of the colleges you're considering to see whether the writing section is required, desirable, optional, or not considered at their school.

 EXTRA POINTER. If due to your financial circumstances it's difficult for you to pay for the SAT or ACT, help is available. Check out HTTPS://SAT.COLLEGEBOARD.ORG/REGISTER/SAT-FEE-WAIVERS for the SAT, and WWW.ACTSTUDENT.ORG/FAQ/FEEWAIVER.HTML for the ACT. At the SAT site you can also get information about which colleges waive the application fee.

5. How many times should I take the test? This is a tough question. In truth, there's no reason to take it more than two or three times, but many students feel pressured to take it over and over. More than three times almost never changes your scores (the testing agencies build the test to intentionally produce similar scores across multiple administrations). Think of it like weight lifting or running: at a certain point you won't get any stronger or any faster no matter how hard you try. With standardized tests, you tend to hit your peak even more quickly.

6. Should I take a test prep class or hire a tutor to help me prepare? It's smart to prepare for your standardized tests, but how you do so is personal preference. Some students can do it all by themselves, some can do it with a friend or teacher, still others need more external motivation via a class or tutor. Just know that when you sign up to take a class or hire a tutor, what you get for your money is 98 percent the same content found in review books, but with much more structure. If you are self-motivated to work through the practice materials on your own, you probably don't need to spend the extra money. Know yourself.

7. How long does it take to get my scores back? Your SAT scores will be posted online within three weeks of the test administration. The ACT score will be posted to a test taker's online account within two and one-half weeks, with the essay score usually added within two weeks after that. (For exact details, for the SAT go to **WWW.SAT.COLLEGEBOARD .ORG/SCORES**, and for the ACT **WWW.ACTSTUDENT.ORG/SCORES**.)

8. Am I required to send all my scores to the schools I apply to? In most cases you can select which test administrations to send to the schools. You can't select individual section scores to send of either the SAT or ACT (e.g. you can't just send your math score), but you can split SAT Subject Tests even taken on one date (in accordance with each school's stated "score-use practice"—check each college's admissions page for policies).

In most cases, rather than stressing out about which tests to include, it's best to just send all the scores. In rare cases, for example, you were sick on test day or were confused about what was going to be on the test, don't feel compelled to send that test score.

EXTRA POINTER. A few highly selective schools require you to send all your test results. This might raise some anxiety, but don't worry. It's in those colleges' best interest to use your highest scores—and they will—when they evaluate your "full testing profile."

9. What is superscoring and will the colleges I apply to superscore my test results? Most colleges superscore standardized tests by creating a composite score of the highest results of individual sections across all administrations, so if you got a 700 on the SAT Math in May but only a 600 in October, they will use the 700 as your score; similarly for the other sections.

Most colleges superscore the SAT. Superscoring the ACT is more complex: some superscore and say so, some do it but don't tell you, and yet still others will not superscore but will evaluate the highest section if it applies to the major you seek.

BEST-KEPT SECRET. Why do colleges superscore? Colleges and universities want to present the highest average testing profile possible to other agencies such as *US News & World Report,* just as you hope to do for your college applications. Superscoring enables them to advertise the "strength" of their admitted class.

ON THE WEB. For a list of which schools superscore—and how they do it—consult HTTPS://PROFESSIONALS.COLLEGEBOARD.COM/ PROFDOWNLOAD/SAT-SCORE-USE-PRACTICES-LIST.PDF.

For a list of some schools that don't, consult WWW.EXAMINER.COM/ARTICLE/COLLEGES-THAT-DO-NOT-SUPERSCORE-THE-SAT.

10. What is the SAT II? While many people call them SAT IIs, the official name of these tests is the SAT Subject Tests. (You'll hear both names used.) SAT Subject Tests are one-hour examinations in particular academic areas, such as math, US History, chemistry, or Spanish. You can take up to three Subject Tests, in any order, on each test date.

11. When should I take the Subject Tests? The best time to take Subject Tests is in the spring, usually as you are finishing up the connected class (i.e. after US History or AP Chemistry). Know that you cannot take the SAT Reasoning Test (usually called the SAT I or just the SAT) and the Subject Tests on the same day. Also, be advised that the foreign language exams with a listening component are only offered in November.

EXTRA POINTER. If you plan on taking both an SAT I: Reasoning Test (that is, SAT) and SAT Subject Tests in the spring, you'll need to plan ahead and split it up. For example, you might take the SAT in May and the SAT Subject Test(s) in June. (Note that the March SAT administration does not offer any Subject Tests.)

12. How many Subject Tests should I take? It depends. Most colleges do not require the Subject Tests at all, although if you can score well it could be in your best interest to send them anyway. If a college asks for Subject Tests, they usually ask for one or two, although a very small number of highly selective schools recommend you submit three. (Note that for some colleges the ACT with writing can be substituted for the SAT plus two Subject Tests.)

13. How should I choose which Subject Tests to take? You should choose your Subject Tests based on your academic strengths and your curriculum or schedule. Most students find they need to be in an honors or AP class to cover all the material they might need for the Subject Test, however. If your curriculum doesn't reach that advanced coursework, consider the Literature or the Math: Level 1 because they are not tied to one particular course but instead assess general skills learned in all math and English classes.

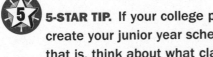

5-STAR TIP. If your college plans include selective schools, create your junior year schedule with SAT Subject Tests in mind, that is, think about what classes you'd need to be able to do well on two Subject Tests. Consider where your strengths lie (math, science, history, etc.) and select an honors or AP class in that field in your junior year.

REALITY CHECK. It's not good to take both the Math 1 and 2 Subject Tests, since colleges would like to see some breadth in your selection of Subject Tests. Also, it's best not to take a language test in a language you speak at home, since colleges will value more a language you learned on your own initiative.

Your Step-by-Step Plan for Preparing for the SAT and ACT

For every college-aspiring student, there's a moment when the standardized test—the ACT, SAT, or both—shows up on the radar screen. When the blip appears on your screen—whether in junior year, sophomore year, or even, for some, freshman year—you'll need to forge a plan for actually preparing for the inevitable. No worries. You'll be fully prepared and at least relatively tension-free if you follow our ten-step plan for getting in gear for the big moment.

STEP 1

Pick your poison. First things first: You need to decide which test to take. If you've taken the Readistep or the PSAT (the SAT's practice tests) or the EXPLORE or PLAN (the ACT's practice tests) you have a pretty good idea of whether you like the SAT or ACT format. If not, weigh the following differences:

- *Timing*: The pre-2016 SAT is longer than the ACT, but this SAT is divided into shorter sections. Case in point: the ACT math section is sixty minutes, but doing a full hour of math could be tiring. The SAT math questions total seventy minutes, but that total is spread among three shorter sections. The 2016 SAT contains longer sections, much like the ACT, but it allows you more time per question than the current ACT.

- *Essay*: The SAT's essay will be required until 2016 and appears at the beginning of the test. The 2016 SAT and the ACT's writing section is optional and appears at the end of the test. So, if you take the 2016 SAT or the ACT's essay, you'll have to keep up your stamina after almost three hours of testing.

- *Content*: The pre-2016 SAT has a greater focus on vocabulary than the 2016 SAT and the ACT. The ACT has a science section, while the SAT does not. And the 2016 SAT's essay requires you to analyze a passage, while the pre-2016 SAT and the ACT ask you to defend your own opinion on an issue.

FLASH! For more information about the changes to the SAT in 2016, see "Big 7 Changes to the 2016 SAT—and What to Do about Them" at the end of this chapter.

STEP 2   **Bookmark the test makers' sites.** Your hub for standardized tests will be either HTTP://SAT.COLLEGEBOARD.ORG (for the SAT) or WWW.ACTSTUDENT.ORG (for the ACT). At these websites you'll be able to get official (and often free) practice material, register for the tests, order optional services, and get your scores after the test. Begin to familiarize yourself with the layout of these sites.

STEP 3   **Subscribe to the Question of the Day.** A little studying each day can go a long way. That's why you should read (and try out) the practice SAT or ACT questions that each test maker gives out every day.

ON THE WEB. The SAT Question of the Day can be found at HTTP://SAT.COLLEGEBOARD.ORG/PRACTICE/SAT-QUESTION-OF-THE-DAY and the ACT Question of the Day is online at WWW.ACT.ORG/QOTD/. The SAT Question of the Day also has an app in the iTunes store as well as a Twitter feed (@SATQuestion).

5-STAR TIP. Keep it official. The SAT and ACT have more than enough practice questions, so there's no need to rely on third-party practice material. Plus, the questions provided by the test makers are going to be most like the questions on the real tests—an added bonus.

STEP 4

Try out the sections. To acquaint yourself with all the parts of the test, you should take a stab at a whole series of questions from each individual part. Read the instructions carefully for each section of the test—you won't want to spend time doing that during the test—then do a block of questions from that particular section. And make sure to try all sections, especially ones you don't feel confident about—that's where the biggest room for score improvement is.

 ON THE WEB. For the SAT, practice questions, complete with instructions, can be found at HTTP://SAT.COLLEGEBOARD.ORG/ PRACTICE/SAT-PRACTICE-QUESTIONS. If you prefer SAT video tutorials (put a face or at least a blackboard to the questions), you'll enjoy the Khan Academy's official questions with explanations: WWW.KHANACADEMY.ORG/SAT. Note that there is separate practice material for the pre-2016 and 2016 SATs–choose appropriately. The ACT practice website can be found at WWW.ACTSTUDENT.ORG/ SAMPLETEST/.

STEP 5

Track down and do an official practice test. Now that you've taken a stab at the test format and the kinds of questions, it's time to crank up the heat and take a full practice test under test conditions. No need to prepare, unless you've been having lots of trouble with the Question of the Day, since this is just a diagnostic exercise, a first stab to see where you stand.

ON THE WEB. A free pre-2016 SAT practice test can be found at HTTP://SAT.COLLEGEBOARD.ORG/PRACTICE/SAT-PRACTICE-TEST; while you're there, download the "Getting Ready for the SAT" guide for even more practice questions. Another full-length SAT test is at WWW.KHANACADEMY.ORG/TEST-PREP/SAT/FULL-LENGTH-SAT-1. Four 2016 SAT practice tests are available at HTTPS:// COLLEGEREADINESS.COLLEGEBOARD.ORG/SAT/PRACTICE/FULL-LENGTH-PRACTICE-TESTS.

A free ACT practice test is available within the "Preparing for the ACT" booklet at WWW.ACT.ORG/AAP/PDF/PREPARING-FOR-THE-ACT.PDF.

EXTRA POINTER. To find other practice tests, scour the Internet; ask a friend, teacher, or counselor; or get *The Official SAT Study Guide* or *The Real ACT Prep Guide* from your library or bookstore.

REALITY CHECK. Any time you prepare for the SAT, make sure you're preparing the questions for that version. You wouldn't want to come in prepared with old, pre-2016 SAT questions only to discover it's already 2016.

STEP 6

Find a smart friend. When it comes to assessing how you did on the practice test, you needn't go it alone. Look for an experienced friend, teacher, or tutor and get him or her to grade your essay and pinpoint your strengths and weaknesses. Pay attention if the person locates systematic problems with your test—say, that you're having problems with algebra, your time management is lacking, or your vocabulary is a little thin. Don't pay overly much attention to the score you get. If you work diligently, your actual test score will be significantly higher.

STEP 7

Brush up on anything you missed. Now's the time to strengthen your weak points with the help of your friend. Depending on what exactly your deficiencies are, you might try doing more practice questions, performing time trials to perfect your time management, studying textbooks or other subject information, or taking additional classes in math, reading, or writing at your school or elsewhere.

REALITY CHECK. Now's the time to decide if you're really ready to take the SAT or ACT at all. It's pointless to take the test if you're missing significant chunks of the material, especially if you're only in tenth or the first semester of eleventh grade (plenty of time left to improve your skills and get a better score).

IOHO. We've never understood why some schools encourage students to take the SAT or ACT each year (three, four, five times in total) with the idea that the more you practice, the better you'll do. You can easily simulate the test taking at home so why sign on to additional stress?

STEP 8

Register for the test (and order QAS, SAS, or TIR). If you decide you're ready for the test, you should sign up about a month or two before you want to take it. When you register, it's well worth coughing up about twenty bucks for the SAT's *Question-and-Answer Service* (QAS) or the ACT's *Test Information Release* (TIR). If you buy one of these, you'll receive back a copy of the questions, your answers, and the right answers some weeks after you take the test. If QAS is not offered for your SAT date, you can still buy the *Student Answer Service* (SAS), which doesn't include the test questions but includes an answer key with your answers. (Though you don't get the questions, the SAS can be helpful in seeing how many questions you got wrong, what sections you missed most points on, whether you had most difficulty with the easier or more difficult questions, and whether there was some time frame in the test in which you did better or worse.)

5-STAR TIP. Check the SAT or ACT websites, HTTP://SAT .COLLEGEBOARD.ORG/SCORES/VERIFY-SAT-SCORES and WWW.ACTSTUDENT .ORG/SCORES/RELEASE.HTML, to see which administrations of the tests include the fuller QAS or TIR reports. If at all possible, aim for these test-taking dates.

STEP 9

Take your second practice test. A week or two before the real test, take another full-length test under test conditions (you know the drill, crank up the heat ...). Having studied like a fiend and having taken the test already once under test conditions, the content and format of the test should be practically second nature—or at least, less surprising and confounding. When finished, again go over this test with your friend, teacher, or tutor.

STEP 10

Take the real test. Follow all the usual standardized test rules: make sure you know where you're going; get a good night's sleep; have a good breakfast; bring your admission ticket, photo ID, #2 pencils, and a watch; keep your cell phone off; and relax. For more tips for taking the test, see "Top 10 SAT/ACT Test-Taking Tips" immediately following.

Top 10 SAT/ACT Test-Taking Tips

You've prepared. You're in the test room. And now you have to face up to the thing. How well you do will depend not only on how well you know your stuff and how good your skills are but also on what strategies you use in actually taking the test. Big improvements can be had if only you know what to do. Here are our 10 best tips for acing the ACT and/or subjugating the SAT:

1. Don't waste a lot of time reading the instructions. Somehow, the SAT and ACT make the simple command "Read each question and pick the right answer" take up paragraphs of wordy prose. If you understand what you need to do in each section, reading the instructions will only waste valuable time. And do you really want to have to puzzle out in the heat of the exam what "If you obtain a decimal answer with more digits than the grid can accommodate, it may be either rounded or truncated, but it must fill the entire grid" means? Certainly not.

 REALITY CHECK. Of course, you'll have gone over the instructions to the various sections as part of your test prep, right?

2. Do the test as written. In the math section, questions that take less time always come first, so be sure to do the questions in numerical order. But in passage-based sections—the pre-2016 SAT Critical Reading section; the 2016 SAT Reading and the Writing and Language sections; and the ACT English, Reading, and Science sections—you should read the passages and inspect the diagrams before reading the questions. Then read the questions before proceeding to the answers. You're trying to narrow down the possible answers by reading the questions and passages, not to narrow down the question by reading the possible answers.

5-STAR TIP. Make sure you fully understand all parts of the question before reading the answers. If you fail to do so, the answers will seem out of context, so you'll be more easily distracted by the wrong ones. If you don't get the question's meaning, make sure to read it again, carefully, until you understand.

3. Work at a brisk pace. The test isn't meant to be a leisurely stroll, but it isn't meant to be the 400m hurdles either. So spend only as much time as is needed to (a) read any passages or diagrams, (b) read the question and understand it fully, (c) work the problem if necessary, (d) read the answers, (e) decide on an answer—and not a moment more. That way, you'll be able to get to each question in the section, and you'll have enough time and mental energy to take a good crack at most of them.

4. Track your time. If your proctor hasn't done so, write down the time the section will end before starting on any questions. Every five questions or so—always between questions—take a look at your watch (phones aren't allowed) and your answer sheet to assess whether you're ahead of the game or behind schedule. Your aim is to speed up incrementally as the time counts down, not to make a mad rush to bubble answers in with seven seconds left on the clock.

EPIC FAIL! On any section that requires reading passages, finishing the second-to-last passage and realizing that you don't have enough time to read the last one is a major error. Even if a particular question is causing problems, realize when it's time to move on by tracking your time as outlined above.

5. Tailor your strategy to the type of question. For sections that don't require referring back to passages, it's best to make a directed search for the answer—that is, to read the question, work the problem, formulate an answer in your mind, and then look to see which (if any) of the possible answers matches your answer. On sections that do require referring back to passages, however, you'll do better by eliminating answers—that is, reading the answers one by one and removing ones that don't fit. That's because on questions about passages, the answers often have fine distinctions, so the process of elimination is likely to be most productive.

EXTRA POINTER. As you read the question, consider covering the answers with your hand if you are making a directed search.

5-STAR TIP. If the given answers ever surprise you or if none of them matches the answer you were thinking of, revert to the process of elimination and work carefully; this is where critical points are won and lost.

6. Avoid too much inner dialectic. If your thoughts are shifting back and forth among the answers—or worse, if you're flitting between the answers, the time remaining, the essay you wrote back in section 1, the problem five questions ahead, and your friend two seats away—you need to refocus your attention on the question at hand. The harder questions require a good deal of concentration, which you can't muster up with your mind on fifty other things.

BEST-KEPT SECRET. If you're torn between, say, answers (b) and (c), deliberate for a few moments but don't linger on the decision. The time could be better spent answering the questions that are not close calls. If you've timed it right, you'll have time to reconsider when you check your work.

7. Never think back. When working on a particular section, never let your thoughts be drawn back to a previous section. Even if you have some sense that you screwed up the math section, you don't really know how you did. And even if you didn't do as well as you could have on some previous section, why get all depressed and mess up this section? That wouldn't make sense.

8. Make sure to guess. On the pre-2016 SAT, you lose $\frac{1}{4}$ of a point for each wrong multiple-choice answer; still, you should always guess if you've read the question. If you are randomly guessing, you gain just as many points, in the long run, by guessing as by just leaving answers blank. If you can eliminate even one answer (and you almost always will be able to), guessing will earn you points over the course of the test. And if you bubble in an answer to each question, rather than leaving a blank row, you won't discover at question 40 that you skipped question 2 and have been filling in answers in the wrong spaces ever since. On the ACT and the 2016 SAT, there's no penalty for guessing, so you definitely don't want to leave answers blank there.

9. Avoid "generally associated withs." Certain wrong answers on the test are meant to attract students who have only understood a part of the question—often the least important part. (These are sometimes called "distractor answers.") For instance, a reading question that asks "What is the best meaning of the word *deliberate* in line 29?" will include some answers that are possible meanings of the word but that don't match the meaning in the passage. Steer clear of these answers by reading the question fully and carefully.

BEST-KEPT SECRET. Certain "generally associated withs" rely on your misreading key words in the questions. So pay special attention to any words such as *except, both, all, not, agree, disagree,* and *only.*

10. Don't put your pencil down before the bitter end. If you have time left, you should always flip back to the start of the section to check your work (especially if there are questions you haven't answered, or circled or starred as ones you weren't sure of). Reread the questions, resolve any close calls, work the problems backwards, and check to make sure everything's bubbled in correctly. A large number of wrong answers can be resolved with a simple check. Why let that opportunity go to waste?

Top 10 Tips for the English Section

The SAT writing section—as well as the ACT English section—tests your knowledge of English grammar and style with multiple-choice questions. Here, you're expected to juggle subjects and verbs, pronouns and antecedents, and restrictive and nonrestrictive clauses as you read intricate sentences and passages. Sound complicated? You'll have no trouble doing good—sorry, we meant well—if you follow our ten best tips.

1. Know what you're being asked to do—and what you're not. As opposed to questions on the reading section (see our "Top 10 Strategies for the Reading Section" for more on this), on the English section you're being asked only about how the passage is written—not on its content. So don't worry about whether the passage is about cars or kazoos; keep your focus on grammar and structure. You'll save both time and mental energy.

EXTRA POINTER. Know the parts specific to your test. The ACT's English section (and starting in 2016, the SAT's Writing and Language section) includes several passages with underlined phrases. You're asked to correct issues of grammar and style by substituting alternative phrases, then to answer some more general questions about the construction and logic of the passage. The pre-2016 SAT's writing section, by contrast, consists of three parts: (1) Improving Sentences, which asks you to correct the underlined portions of single sentences (just like the ACT, only no passages); (2) Identifying Sentence Errors, which asks you to either pick out the error in a sentence or state that no error exists (nothing like this on the ACT); and (3) Improving Paragraphs, which poses questions about a short, imperfectly written passage (somewhat like the ACT, only the questions come at the end of the paragraph, thus encouraging you to read the entire paragraph before attempting the questions). The tip? Familiarize yourself with the format of your English section—and its peculiarities and rules—as part of your preparation.

---

2. Acquaint yourself with basic grammatical principles. Many of the questions on the English section can be answered by using a few grammatical principles.

- *Subject-verb agreement*. Singular subjects take singular verbs, ditto for plural subjects and verbs.

- *Pronoun case*. If the pronoun is acting as a subject (performing an action), it needs to be nominative (I, he, she, we, they). Otherwise, it should be objective (me, him, her, us, them).

- *Verb tense*. Verbs in different parts of a sentence or passage have to agree with one another.

- *Adjective/adverb confusion*. If it describes a noun, it needs to be an adjective. Otherwise, it needs to be an adverb (usually ending in *-ly*).

- *Fragments*. Each sentence needs to have a subject and a verb.

- *Parallelism*. Words, phrases, and clauses joined by conjunctions should have similar grammatical constructions.

- *Misplaced modifiers*. Any phrases or clauses that describe anything should be placed close to whatever they're describing.

- *Passive voice*. Usually, the subject of the sentence should perform the action stated.

3. Read out loud during practice. It's best to have a sense of sound: that is, when a sentence is wrong, it should simply sound odd. To develop this sense, read the sentences and passages in practice questions out loud. If you stumble while reciting the sentence, that's a sign that an error might be near. This especially helps you identify sentences that are awkward or confusing. (In the test, you won't be able to read out loud, of course, but for difficult sentences on which you're stumped, you might be able to read them to yourself silently, imagining the sound of the words and sentences.)

4. Mark up sentences. As you practice—and even as you take the test—feel free to write on the sentences and passages to aid your understanding. Draw arrows connecting subjects to their verbs, pronouns to their antecedents, and descriptive words and phrases to the words they're describing. Also, use arrows to move around sentences and paragraphs for questions that ask you to rearrange parts of a passage.

5. Read sentence-by-sentence, not word-by-word. Consider the sentence, "The hiring policy of the top Fortune 500 companies are strict." Here, the subject ("policy") and the verb ("are") are far away from each other, and you might not notice the error if you read in small chunks. To help you spot more of these errors, read in full sentences—not one word or phrase at a time.

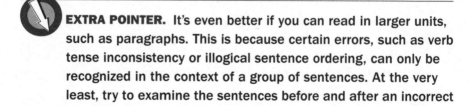

EXTRA POINTER. It's even better if you can read in larger units, such as paragraphs. This is because certain errors, such as verb tense inconsistency or illogical sentence ordering, can only be recognized in the context of a group of sentences. At the very least, try to examine the sentences before and after an incorrect sentence when you think they might shed light on the error.

5-STAR TIP. When you need to reword an underlined phrase (on the 2016 SAT, on the ACT, or in the Improving Sentences or the Improving Paragraphs parts of the pre-2016 SAT), be sure to read the answer choices in the context of the entire sentence by substituting them into the sentence.

6. Make a note the moment you spot an error. Sometimes, you will see an obvious grammatical mistake in the passage or in one of the answer choices. Immediately mark the error so that you'll know to rule that answer out (or, in the case of the pre-2016 SAT's Identifying Sentence Errors part, to consider selecting that answer). Still, make sure to read to the end of that answer choice (as well as all the other answer choices) before bubbling in your final answer. A later part of the phrase might render correct what you thought was an error.

7. Recognize the difference between grammatical and stylistic errors. A *grammatical* error flagrantly violates one of the laws of standard written English, such as the rule against comma splices (e.g., "This is a good tip, it will really work."). On the other hand, *stylistic* errors, such as awkwardness and wordiness, make sentences sound bad. A grammatical error is stronger than a stylistic one. That is, between an answer choice with an error in grammar and an answer choice with an error in style, you should choose a stylistic error as correct. Stylistic errors can be defended but grammatical errors are always wrong.

BEST-KEPT SECRET. The errors on the pre-2016 SAT's Identifying Sentence Errors part are almost always *grammatical*. Don't be fooled by slightly unusual sentence constructions, and don't be afraid to choose "no error" if the only possible problems in the sentence are those of style.

---

8. Be aware of SAT- and ACT-specific errors. Each of the two tests includes some grammatical principles that you might not have learned. On the SAT, these include the following:

•*Errors in comparison*. No comparing apples to oranges. For example, "The beliefs of John Locke were more refined than his friends," is wrong (we're comparing "beliefs" to "friends"). It should be, "The beliefs of John Locke were more refined than those of his friends."

•*Errors in idiom*. Certain words require specific prepositions. For example, "I am attracted for science" is wrong; "I am attracted to science" is right.

The ACT and the 2016 SAT prefer to test the following:

•*Punctuation*. Know when to use punctuation, especially commas. For example, the sentence "A ball you thought was lost, inexplicably bounces back into play." embodies a punctuation error—the comma after "lost." (Immediately mark the error, following tip 6 above.)

•*Redundancy*. Don't say the same thing multiple times. For example, "I had an epiphany, which turned out to be revealing," is redundant because an epiphany, by definition, is revealing. Simply say, "I had an epiphany."

•*Tone*. All sentences in the passage should have the same, preferably clear and formal, tone. For example, the sentence "The Constitution is an important foundational document" is preferable to "The Constitution is a pretty big deal." On the other hand, the sentence "The Constitution is a hoary testimony to our liberty" imports needlessly complicated (and imprecise) language.

•*Distracting sentences*. Make sure all the sentences support the main idea of the passage.

9. On the 2016 SAT and the ACT, make two sweeps through the passage. The passage-based English questions on these tests come in two types: those that are contained within one sentence and those that rely on your knowledge of the sentences surrounding a given sentence. As the ACT's instructions put it, "For many of the questions, you must read several sentences beyond the question to determine the answer." Your best strategy is to read the passage once, answering all the questions that are self-contained. Then go back over the passage and polish off the rest of them.

10. On the pre-2016 SAT's Identifying Sentence Errors part, test the choices as you read. When you have to find an error in a sentence—as you do on Identifying Sentence Errors—try to examine each possible error as you read it. If a verb is underlined as a possible error, ask yourself, "Does this verb agree with the subject? Is it the right tense?" If a pronoun is underlined, ask yourself, "Does this pronoun refer to the correct noun? Is the pronoun in the correct case?" Using this technique, not only can you find the true error faster but also you can rule out answers (as containing no error) more effectively. And, having fewer answers to choose from is always helpful.

Top 10 Tips to Make Yourself a Mathmagician (or at least Kill the Math Section)

For many students, the math section is the most intimidating section of the SAT or ACT. While it may seem simple enough to read passages or find errors in sentences, when it comes to calculating the surface area of a complex polyhedron while racing against the clock—well, that's enough to make even the most experienced test taker sweat buckets. You'll have the time of your life doing the math questions—both the garden-variety, multiple-choice questions and, on the SAT, the student-produced "grid-ins"—if you follow our 10 tips for making the math section as easy as pie (or pi).

1. Get on top of the concepts. Before the test, look on the web to find out exactly what kinds of math you'll be tested on—not only whole subjects such as algebra, geometry, and trigonometry but also micro-concepts such as probability and average speed. Then, sit down with a math teacher or savvy friend and work some practice problems, identifying each by the concept tested. Make sure that your helper explains not only why you got the problem wrong (if you did) but also any related concepts. So, for example, if you don't understand a question about 45°-45°-90° triangles, make sure you learn not just the properties of those triangles but also the properties of related triangles such as the 30°-60°-90° triangle. Then, test out your newly acquired knowledge by applying it to still other problems.

 ON THE WEB. For a list of concepts tested on the pre-2016 SAT, use *The SAT Mathematics Review,* which can be found at HTTP:// PROFESSIONALS.COLLEGEBOARD.COM/PROFDOWNLOAD/SAT-MATHEMATICS-REVIEW.PDF.

Find practice problems, separated by overall concept (for example, "number and operations," "algebra and functions," "geometry and measurement," "data analysis, statistics, and probability"), at HTTP://SAT.COLLEGEBOARD.ORG/PRACTICE/SAT-PRACTICE-QUESTIONS-MATH/MATH-CONCEPTS.

And be sure to try the Question of the Day and deal your friend in by using the "Challenge a Friend" box—they'll love you for that.

The ACT concept description can be found at WWW.ACTSTUDENT.ORG/TESTPREP/DESCRIPTIONS/MATHCONTENT.HTML; topics here include three levels of algebra (pre-, elementary, and intermediate) and coordinate and plane geometry.

ACT problem sets are to be had at WWW.ACTSTUDENT.ORG/SAMPLETEST/MATH/MATH_01.HTML.

For more information on the 2016 SAT's math section—and how it differs from the current one—see the section "Flash! Big 7 Changes to the 2016 SAT—and What to Do about Them" at the end of this chapter.

 RULE OF THUMB. No number of practice problems is too many unless you're getting most all of them right.

---

2. Master what your math teachers didn't teach you. Some of the tested topics—for instance, basic statistics, set theory, basic number theory, combinations, and permutations—might not have been fully covered in your math classes (either because your teachers didn't have time to get to them, because your teachers didn't consider them all that important, or perhaps even because they didn't realize they'd be on the test). As you review the concepts (as described in the previous tip), pay special attention to these topics, which can yield a number of questions on the actual exam.

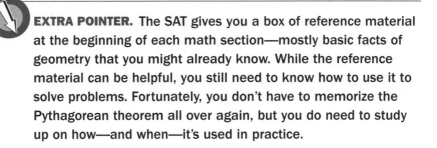

IOHO. Topics on the pre-2016 SAT are usually taught in Algebra 1, Geometry, and Algebra 2 classes; the ACT, as well as the 2016 SAT, requires a bit of trigonometry as well. We recommend that you take all these classes before attempting the tests so that you're not playing with less than a full deck of math skills. Why get needlessly depressed with a lowball score when you haven't even learned the material being tested?

3. Brush up on your math vocabulary and symbols. For many questions, it's important that the answer is an integer, or is greater than (>) rather than less than (<) a given quantity, or relates to an equilateral triangle. As you prepare for the test, make note of any words or symbols that you don't completely or correctly understand and resolve to look them up. This simple step will both save time and improve your performance on the test.

EXTRA POINTER. The SAT gives you a box of reference material at the beginning of each math section—mostly basic facts of geometry that you might already know. While the reference material can be helpful, you still need to know how to use it to solve problems. Fortunately, you don't have to memorize the Pythagorean theorem all over again, but you do need to study up on how—and when—it's used in practice.

4. Symbolize the problem as you read it. For each sentence of some word problems, rewrite the sentence using the language of algebra and geometry. For instance, "two added to x is less than or equal to y" can be rewritten as $2 + x \leq y$. Similarly, if the question reads "The fraction of books that Bob has read is twice the fraction of books that Bob has not read," translate to $R = 2(1 - R)$ (where R is the fraction that Bob has read). When you simplify that to $R = \left(\frac{2}{3}\right)$, you have solved for one variable already and are on your way to solving the problem as a whole. Or, if you're given an unlabeled geometric diagram together with some facts about it, it's a good idea by mark them on the diagram using generally accepted geometrical symbolism (for instance, drawing tick marks on two lines means those lines are congruent).

5. Consider different mathematical strategies. Unlike in your math classes, on this test you are allowed to use whatever method you like to solve the problem; no teacher is standing over you, requiring you to use, say, the quadratic formula to solve polynomials. So consider the following methods and choose the best and fastest to solve the problem: *analytical* (solving the equation, factoring the expression, or finding the answer using standard mathematical methods); *graphical* (generating a graph on paper or with your graphing calculator and working with it); *guess and check* (trying out different values until you hit on the right one); *eliminating answers* (ruling out choices that don't make mathematical or practical sense); and *working backwards from the possible answers* (trying each in turn till you find one, or more, that works).

 5-STAR TIP. Learn to use your calculator. Students who have incomplete mastery of their calculator—or worse, sidestep it altogether—often get lower scores than their more techie classmates. For tips on how best to use your calculator, see "7 Things You Need to Know about Your Calculator (but Might Not)," immediately following this section.

6. Avoid using brute force. One strategy you never want to use is trying to enumerate or test every possibility. For example, a question that asks you how many ways is something possible should be solved by using permutations, combinations, counting principles, or logic, not by listing out all the possible ways. (The last is a major time-waster and, sometimes, the enumeration can't even be completed.)

7. Substitute numbers for variables. If you see a question such as "if x is a multiple of 3, what must be true about $3x-7$?," you should first pick a particular value for the variable x that satisfies the given condition (for example, 9, which is a multiple of 3); then calculate the value of the whole expression substituting the value you have selected (in this case, $3(9) - 7 = 20$); and finally, check the possible answers for one(s) that are true of your result (for example, choice (b), "is 2 more than a multiple of 3"). Keep in mind that if two (or more) answers apply, you will have to substitute additional values for x in order to narrow down the answer to a unique one of the choices provided.

EXTRA POINTER. Be careful when choosing which numbers you substitute. If the question states that "a is an even number that is not a perfect square," 16 would be a bad choice for a test value of a (it's a perfect square). And just because a property is true of one value doesn't mean that it must be true for all values, so be careful when facing any question with the word *must*.

8. Keep your options open. You'll occasionally see questions like "which of these is a possible value of x, given certain conditions?" Be sure you've considered the full range of possibilities. For example, if x is found by performing operations on a certain number y, keep in mind that the number y can be positive, negative, fractional, even, or odd. If x is a length AB, make sure to consider the possibility that A is to the right of B, not just to the left. And if x relates to a data set, be sure to realize that numbers added to the set can be greater than or less than the numbers already in the set.

9. Check your answer immediately after each problem. In other sections, it's often a good idea to check your answer only at the end of the section because you'll find mistakes more easily if you look at the question with fresh eyes. On the math section, though, you should perform a short check just after you finish the problem, working the problem backwards or in a different way. This is because you'll want to save the last few minutes of the section to tie up the harder problems, not to recheck the easier ones. The earlier you realize that you wrote + instead of −, the more time you'll save overall.

10. For the SAT, learn the rules for grid-ins before you take the test. Some of the SAT math questions (on both the pre-2016 and 2016 versions) have no given answers, so it's up to you to figure out the answer and enter it on a special grid. The rules for gridding the answers seem daunting at first look, so understand them before you face them on the real test. Some highlights:

What you fill in the circles, not in the boxes, will be scored.

You must fill the grid if you get a long decimal (round 0.03125 to .031, not .03).

Mixed numbers cannot be gridded (4 $\frac{1}{4}$ will be interpreted as $\frac{41}{4}$, which is wrong), but need to be converted to an improper fraction or a decimal ($\frac{17}{4}$ or 4.25).

 ON THE WEB. Get all the gridding instructions, fill in some practice grids, and try a few grid-in questions at HTTP://SAT .COLLEGEBOARD.ORG/PRACTICE/SAT-PRACTICE-QUESTIONS-MATH/STUDENT-PRODUCED-RESPONSE.

---

7 Things You Need to Know about Your Calculator (but Might Not)

Good knowledge of a graphing calculator can really boost your chances of success on the SAT or ACT math section. (Note, however, that the 2016 SAT includes a noncalculator math section, in addition to a math section in which calculator use is permitted.) Although you never need to use your calculator to solve a problem, effective use of your calculator can save time and greatly decrease your chance of mistakes (thus almost surely giving your score a boost). Not quite sure how to tap your calculator's full potential? Have a look at the 7 things you need to know about your calculator—but probably don't.

1. The more experience you have with it, the better your calculator will work for you. While most everyone has an opinion on which calculator is the best, the best calculator for you is the one you have the most experience with. So buy a calculator ASAP (if you don't already have one), work with it for as long as you can, feel free to explore the menus and buttons to see what they do, and try to use your calculator knowledge to solve and check math problems.

 REALITY CHECK. Almost all high school math courses require a graphing calculator—as the name suggests, a calculator with the ability to generate graphs of functions. The most popular brand is Texas Instruments (models include the TI-84 and TI-Nspire), and others include Casio and HP. While graphing calculators are more expensive and complex, we recommend them over scientific and four-function calculators because of their added functionality and their ease of use.

ON THE WEB. A simple web search for "best graphing calculators" or "best graphing calculators for the SAT (or ACT)" will net lots of good information, comparisons, and rankings. One site we like is HTTP://GRAPHING-CALCULATOR-REVIEW .TOPTENREVIEWS.COM/.

BEST-KEPT SECRET. If you're not game to spend $100+ on a calculator, consider buying a used one, often at less than half the price, at Amazon or on eBay.

2. Your calculator is best used for the last step in a problem. You should never use the calculator unless you have a clear idea of what you hope to get out of using it—in almost all cases, you will use the calculator to produce the final answer. The tasks of writing equations, recognizing relationships, and understanding which steps to use should all take place before you turn your calculator on. Using your calculator from the very start of a problem, with no real idea what you're looking for, is more likely to be a time-waster than a time-saver.

EXTRA POINTER. Even if you didn't use your calculator to find the answer, you should consider using it to check your answer. For example, if you find that a certain value should satisfy an equation, you could calculate each side of the equation with that value and verify that they do in fact equal one another.

3. Your calculator is sensitive to small details. It's very easy to make subtle mistakes while using your calculator. Two of the most common are

- Misplaced parentheses: 2/3x means $\frac{2}{3}x$, while 2/(3x) means $\frac{2}{3x}$;

•Confusing radian and degree modes: when using trigonometric functions such as sine, cosine, and tangent, and the measures of angles are in degrees (e.g., 85°), your calculator must be in degree mode; if angle measures are in radians (e.g., $\frac{\pi}{3}$), your calculator must be in radian mode. On many calculators, you can switch between modes in the MODE menu, but read your calculator's manual to get more specifics.

4. Your calculator has lots of additional functions that you don't know about (yet). Forget addition, subtraction, multiplication, and division—your calculator likely can change fractions to decimals (and vice versa), can calculate the greatest common factor and least common multiple, can calculate permutations and combinations, and much more. If there aren't buttons for these functions, they can often be found in the MATH menu.

EXTRA POINTER. Realize the differences between the notation you use in math class and the notation your calculator uses. On some models, what you might write as $\sqrt[4]{64}$ is written 4 x$\sqrt{}$64. Newer operating systems are getting better at writing operations in more typical ways.

5. Your calculator assigns two functions to each key. Just like the shift key on your computer keyboard allows you to access a second character on many keys (for example, the number keys), so too the 2ND key on your calculator provides access to a second function (press the 2ND key then the relevant function key; this second function is written in small letters above the key.) In addition, a number of keys have a third item, A-Z and some Greek letters and punctuation marks, which are accessed by pressing the ALPHA key and then the relevant button. These are used for storing numbers to variables.

6. Your calculator allows you to store numbers as variables. If you're doing a multistep calculation and have found an answer of 1.414213562 for the first part, instead of copying out all 10 digits in the second part of the calculation, you can store 1.414213562 to a variable, such as *A*. When you then type in *A* in the next step of the problem, the calculator will automatically substitute the value—much easier than typing in the long string of numbers and, what's more, the calculator isn't going to get confused and leave off numbers. On some calculators, you store 1.414213562 to A by typing in *1.414213562 STO> A*.

5-STAR TIP. Similarly, you can use the ANS key to place the answer of the previous calculation into the next calculation. For example, if the answer to your last calculation was 3, and you want to find the sine of 3, typing sin(ANS) will yield the same result as sin(3). Using ENTRY (just above ENTER on most calculators; use the keystroke combination 2ND ENTER to access this) or the up arrow in conjunction with ENTER will allow you to repeat previous calculations, thus saving valuable typing time.

7. Your (graphing) calculator can graph functions and make tables. Go to the Y= menu (or equivalent), enter a function using x (typically found on the key marked X, T, Θ, n), and hit GRAPH or TABLE to get, well, a graph or table. Using the CALC menu (typically accessed by pressing 2ND and then TRACE), you can find the value of a function at a certain point, calculate the maximum or minimum value of a function, find the zeroes of a function, and calculate the intersection point of two functions. This makes equation solving very simple. To find where $2x+3 = (x+2)2$, graph each side of the equation in your calculator and use the CALC features to find where the two graphs intersect.

BEST-KEPT SECRET. If you want to see a graph and do other calculations at the same time, some calculators have a split-screen option in the MODE menu, in the row starting with FULL. HORIZ presents a graph in the upper half of the screen and a calculation window in the lower half, and G – T presents a graph on the left side of the screen and a table on the right side. Pretty cool.

BONUS TIP. Your calculator can be mastered (if you put your mind to it). Just about now you might be thinking: What is all this stuff? How's a mere mortal supposed to figure out how to do all these things? Relax. If you haven't quite gotten your mind around all these suggestions, find a friend or teacher who will help you understand just what to do. And, if you want to puzzle the stuff out on your own, a good start is the instruction manual for your particular calculator.

For Texas Instruments calculators, guidebooks can be found at HTTP://EDUCATION.TI.COM/EN/US/DOWNLOADS-AND-ACTIVITIES? ACTIVE=GUIDEBOOKS.

For Casio calculators, the link is HTTP://SUPPORT.CASIO.COM/ EN/MANUAL/MANUALLIST.PHP?CID=004.

Finally, HP calculators offer manuals at HTTP://H20180.WWW2 .HP.COM/APPS/LOOKUP?H_PAGETYPE=S-003&H_CLIENT=Z-A-R1002--3&H_ PAGE=INDEX&H_LANG=EN&H_CC=US&JUMPID=HPR_R1002_USEN_LINK1.

Top 10 Strategies for the Reading Section

For many students, the reading sections of the SAT and ACT embody all that's difficult about standardized tests. Shades of meaning, hard-to-follow passages, blanks that don't quite fill in right, vocabulary you've never even heard of—all of these conspire to make even the most devoted test taker nervous. And yet, even a modicum of strategy for the Critical Reading section on the pre-2016 SAT or the Reading section on the 2016 SAT and on the ACT—and the special sentence completions that appear on the pre-2016 SAT only—will get you over the hump and reading with the best. Skeptical? Have a look at our ten best tips for acing the reading section.

1. Always read the entire passage first. Few of the reading section questions deal with small parts of the passage; even the ones that focus on a specific sentence often ask you to relate it to the passage as a whole. For this reason, you need to have a good sense of the whole passage before you complete the questions. Upshot? Start working on the questions only after you've read the passage completely.

 EXTRA POINTER. Always read the little introduction at the beginning of the passage (italicized on the pre-2016 SAT, in small type on the 2016 SAT and ACT). These few words sometimes tell you what the passage is saying or provide context that'll help you get the point of what you're about to read.

2. Read at a comfortable pace. You might be tempted to skim the passage, especially if time is beginning to be a factor. But if you read too fast, you won't understand the passage as well, and you'll lose time rereading the sections you didn't understand the first time around. As you read, make sure that you understand every sentence of the passage. If you don't, slow down.

3. Track the progress of the passage as you read. As you make your way through the passage, try to develop a sense of the main idea of the passage—the point the author is trying to convey—and the direction of the passage—the argument and evidence the author uses to support the main idea. Many questions will ask about these concepts, and the best time to internalize them is while you're reading.

5-STAR TIP. To analyze the passage, ask yourself these questions as you read: *What is the author trying to argue? What is the purpose of this paragraph? How does this paragraph build on the previous ones? What conclusions does the author draw?* Some students find it helpful to mark up the passage as they read: underline or circle any sentences that state main points, draw arrows when a paragraph references an earlier or later paragraph (or contrasts with a second passage, if there are two), or write brief key words in the margins to describe each part of the argument.

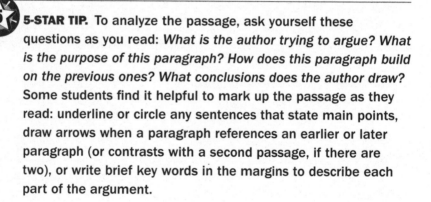

EXTRA POINTER. You might think that only persuasive essays have main ideas and supporting evidence. However, narrative passages (those that tell a story or develop a character) have main ideas as well, which usually are insights about life (a theme) or about a character. Narrative passages also have evidence, usually in the form of dialogue, actions, or narration that supports the main idea.

4. Locate the author's position. Authors usually take a stand on several issues during a passage. As you read, keep a mental list of what the author agrees and disagrees with. Also, keep track of the author's attitude toward certain subjects: for example, an author who uses the phrase "this so-called science" when discussing economics probably views economics negatively. For narrative passages, note whether the narrator is one of the characters or an impartial observer, and try to find the narrator's view toward the characters and events.

BEST-KEPT SECRET. For many arguments, the author's position is more complicated than, say, "pro-nature" or "anti-nature." The author might support efforts to preserve nature only in certain cases or might believe that natural land is beneficial but not productive. Look for nuanced, not just yes/no, positions.

EPIC FAIL! Don't confuse a view the author is trying to refute with his or her own opinion.

5. Figure out the relationships between two related passages. Some parts of the reading section test your understanding of pairs of passages. In these cases, try to assess how the passages relate: *Are they in direct opposition or do the authors hold compatible opinions? Are there any statements that both authors would agree on? Is there any material in one passage that would rebut material from the other passage?* The better you connect the passages as you read, the easier it'll be to answer the questions that test these connections.

6. Look back to individual sentences—and their surrounding context. Many reading questions, such as "What is the purpose of line 5?", include a reference to a line in the passage. Since you can't rely on each line to explain itself, reread not only the referenced line (in this case, line 5) but also the lines surrounding it. Often, the sentences before and after the line explicitly state its purpose or clarify its role in the passage; therefore, they are the ones that will help you the most.

 EXTRA POINTER. Don't see the referenced lines in a vacuum. Use your mental or written notes you made while reading to provide even more context. If, for instance, the question asks how the author feels about a term used in a specific line, use your knowledge about the author's position to deduce his or her attitude.

7. Justify your answers to yourself. The reading section requires more judgment than many of the other sections. Therefore, try to find lines in the passage that back up the answers you choose and that refute the answers you did not choose. If you can't find enough evidence for an answer, consider choosing another.

 EXTRA POINTER. Sometimes an answer is wrong simply because no evidence from the passage supports it. For example, if there were no indication that the author supported equal rights, that would be enough to make the answer "Paragraph 2 proves the author supports equal rights" incorrect.

 BEST-KEPT SECRET. When you're preparing, jot down the line numbers that support your answer. Then flip to the answer explanations (found in most test prep books and online resources) and see which lines the test makers cite. If your evidence matches theirs, you did a good job working through the question; otherwise, look back at your rationale to see if you did anything wrong.

FLASH! The 2016 SAT includes many questions that specifically ask you to cite a line that backs up your answer. Just another reason to explain your answers to yourself.

8. For vocabulary in the context of a passage, substitute the options into the passage. Some questions ask you what a particular word in a passage means. An example is "In line 50, 'distinct' most nearly means what?" For these questions, you need to substitute the answer choices into the line because each answer choice is usually a plausible meaning of the word in itself. For instance, "distinct" means "clear" in the sentence, "He had a distinct idea of his career goals," but "distinct" means "separate" in the sentence, "Philosophy and science are two distinct fields."

9. For pre-2016 SAT sentence-completion questions, pay attention to connectives and descriptive phrases. Words such as "although" and "because" will help you figure out the meaning of the omitted word. For instance, the twin connectives "although" and "actually" in the sentence, "Although one would expect the TV host to be gregarious, his behavior was actually_____," show that the omitted word is the opposite of "gregarious." (Since "gregarious" means "friendly," the omitted word must mean "unfriendly.") Similarly, phrases that describe the omitted words can help you. An example of this is, "The newspaper's op-ed was_____ but _____: that is, short but intense." Here, the omitted words must be synonyms of "short" and "intense," respectively.

EXTRA POINTER. It's good to have an idea of the meaning of the omitted word before you move through the answers. Knowing what you're looking for makes it easier to find.

10. For two-blank pre-2016 SAT sentence-completion questions, treat each blank separately. Some sentence-completion questions contain two blanks. On these questions, focus on just one blank to start; go through the answers and rule out any one that fills in that blank incorrectly. Then move to the other blank and work through the answers that remain. This technique saves time and enables you to get the answer without knowing all the words in each answer choice.

5-STAR TIP. It's sometimes useful to start by filling in the second blank. If you know what has to go there, the choices for the first blank often reduce to two—sometimes direct opposites of each other.

EXTRA POINTER. For sentence completions, don't pick the oddest word for no reason. If you don't know all the words in the answers, try to make an educated guess. This could be based on related words (for example, "mercurial" sounds like "mercury") or, for language aficionados, Greek or Latin roots. Try, though, not to make a guess simply on the basis of the length or complexity of the word.

The Science of Taking the Science Section on the ACT

They say it's a "40-question, 35-minute test that measures the skills required in the natural sciences: interpretation, analysis, evaluation, reasoning, and problem solving." It's the science section, unique to the ACT and not part of the SAT. But it turns out it's more a question of carefully reading charts and graphs and processing the information already there. So even if you're not an Einstein, Newton, or Faraday—and even if you're not doing so hot in your Earth Science, Physical Science, and Biology courses (supposed prerequisites for the ACT)—you can still ace the science section. How so? Follow our nine highest value tips (and put your fear of science to bed).

1. Remain calm. The science section, with its array of technical terms, obscure graphs, and complicated diagrams, can look like a daunting enterprise. Indeed, most students' first reaction when looking over a sample test is "OMG, how am I ever going to do this?" But relax. The science section is at base only a reading test: you're given what you need to know to solve the problems, so little substantial previous knowledge of science is actually necessary.

 5-STAR TIP. Many times, passages in the science section begin with a longish, descriptive introductory paragraph. Don't panic if you don't fully have your mind around what's being said. Usually, the tables and graphs that follow explain the experiments and situations more clearly than the introductory paragraphs do. Be sure to have a look at the tables and graphs and see what's going on there before moving to the questions.

2. Move back and forth within each passage. There's a lot to keep track of as you move through this test, so you should move freely among the questions, the tables and graphs, and the introductory paragraphs at the beginning of each section. After reading a question, refer back to the passage and its tables and graphs to answer. Then double-check your answer using the original question.

 5-STAR TIP. Keep your main focus on the tables and graphs. Most questions can be answered using only *one* table or graph, so locate the relevant table or graph as soon as you've read the question. Some harder questions require two sources of information: a pair of graphs or one graph and the introductory paragraphs. If you find you can't fully answer the question after consulting one graph, look for its partner.

3. Use the clues. Most of the easier questions will say something like, "According to Figure 1 …" or "Based on the results of Experiments 2 and 3 …" These phrases are meant to guide you to the correct tables, graphs, and descriptions. If the question asks for Table 1, don't waste time on Tables 2 and 3; only use the information the ACT asks you to use.

 EPIC FAIL! Don't misread the number of the referenced figure or table. It's easy to do, and will not only guarantee you a wrong answer but will waste enormous amounts of time in the process.

4. Keep track of what's changing—and what isn't. For each experiment, make sure you know what quantity is being measured (the dependent variable), what quantity is being varied (the independent variable), and which quantities do not change (the constants). For example, if you are measuring the effect of heat on bean plant growth, the growth rate would be the dependent variable (that's what's being measured); the heat added to the plant would be the independent variable (it is being varied); and the type of plant, bean plant, would be a constant (it remains the same).

BEST-KEPT SECRET. Track changes across experiments. When you read about multiple experiments, note whether the independent variable, the dependent variable, or both are changing. Some questions will test you on these changes.

REALITY CHECK. If you have no idea what we're talking about, try to see your science teacher. He or she should be happy to answer a few specific questions about variables and experiments.

5. Track relationships between variables. As you read through tables and graphs, take note of how one variable relates to the other. Some relations include a positive correlation (as one variable increases, the other does, too) and a negative correlation (as one variable decreases, the other increases). It's also possible that one variable has no effect on the other; that is, one variable stays constant as the other increases or decreases. Many questions ask—either directly or indirectly—about these relationships, so you should be sure you have a good grasp on these concepts.

EXTRA POINTER. On a graph, a positive correlation will look like a diagonal line from the lower left to the upper right. A negative correlation will look like a diagonal line from the upper left to the lower right. Finally, if one variable does not affect the other, the graph will look like a horizontal line.

6. Pay particular attention to labels and units. Tables and graphs will usually show a number of different variables. Therefore, you should always read the labels on the top row of a table or along the sides and bottom of a graph before you look at the table or graph.

The units that accompany the labels won't always mean much to you (who knows what a millibar is, anyway?), but you can often check the units in the answers against the units in the table. Use common sense too: if the question asks for length, the table giving values in degrees Celsius is not the one for you.

7. Be prepared for hypotheticals. The last question in many passages involves a hypothetical situation: for instance, if we used a stronger metal rod here, how would the weight needed to displace the rod change? These questions (thought by many students to be the hardest part of the science section) test your understanding of the conceptual framework of the experiment by asking you to apply it to a new case. Reread the introductory material and determine the immediate effects of the hypothetical change (e.g., if the metal rod were stronger, more force would be needed to displace it in all circumstances).Then determine how the change would affect the requested measurement (e.g., to provide more force, the weight needed to displace the rod would increase in all circumstances).

8. Use your scientific knowledge. Occasionally a question will ask for a fact that you already know ("According to Table 1, which atom contains the fewest electrons?"). If you're lucky enough to get such a question, just answer according to what you know. If you don't know the fact, that's fine, too; remember that all the answers are just waiting to be found in the tables, graphs, and introductory material.

EXTRA POINTER. You might see a few questions that demand some knowledge of general science and cannot be answered simply by looking at the introductory material. If you see these in a practice test, consult the answer explanations to get a review of the science concept being tested. And if you see these on the actual test, rule out answers you know are false, consider which answers would agree with the given information, and make an educated guess.

9. For "dueling passages," pay attention to differences in justification. Each science section will contain a passage in which two or more scientists disagree on an issue. Sometimes they're disagreeing not about what's happening, the phenomenon in question, but rather why it's happening, that is, the reason or explanation for the occurrence. For instance, one scientist might attribute increased cloud formation to warmer temperatures, whereas the other might attribute this cloud formation to higher humidity. Make note of how the scientists differ in their assessment of events and in their explanation of these events and consider how these differences would affect their outlook on other scientific issues.

BONUS TIP. Stay focused and on track. The ACT science section has a total of six passages—two more than on the ACT reading section. So make sure to move to the next passage about every five minutes. Stay focused, too—although it's the last section on the test, the science section is still worth one-fourth of your ACT score. Why squander that?

10 Best Tips for Writing the SAT/ACT Essay

Many students fear the essay section of the pre-2016 SAT or the optional Writing Test on the ACT. In this section of the test, you're given a topic (called a "prompt"). On the pre-2016 SAT, you might get the question "Is it better to make snap judgments, instead of reasoned decisions?" You then have to develop your opinion and present it in a well-written essay—all in about half an hour. On the ACT–which has just changed–it's a little different. You're given three perspectives on a controversial contemporary issue (for example, personal freedom vs. societal good), then asked to analyze and evaluate each of the views, connecting them to your own personal opinion. Either way, you'll write a great essay if you follow our 10 best tips.

 REALITY CHECK. The optional essay section of the 2016 SAT is also a little different; for a fuller description, consult "Flash! Big 7 Changes to the 2016 SAT—and What to Do about Them" as well as the more general tips in the section you're now reading.

1. Know what counts. Two readers will examine your essay and assign it a score (on the SAT) or multiple scores (on the ACT). In general, your readers will look for how you state and argue your opinion (or viewpoint or position), including what evidence you include; the organization of your essay; how well you focus all parts of your essay around your viewpoint; your choice of words and phrases; how you vary your sentence structure; and the grammar of your essay. Once you know what your reader is looking for, you'll be able to construct your essay accordingly.

ON THE WEB. The pre-2016 SAT's essay scoring guide can be found at HTTP://SAT.COLLEGEBOARD.ORG/SCORES/SAT-ESSAY-SCORING-GUIDE, and the ACT's writing scoring guidelines are online at WWW.ACTSTUDENT.ORG/WRITING/SCORES/GUIDELINES.HTML. At both those sites you'll be able to find sample essays that received each of the possible scores. Very much worth a look.

 REALITY CHECK. If you're taking the pre-2016 SAT, remember that the essay only comprises about 30 percent of the larger writing score; the remaining 70 percent comes from how well you answer the multiple-choice grammar questions. Proportion your angst accordingly. And on the 2016 SAT or the ACT, remember that the essay is completely optional, unless a college you're applying to requires it.

2. Hit the ground running. After carefully reading the prompt, you might be inclined to plan or outline your essay. Remember, though, that if you spend even ten minutes planning, you've wasted at least 25 percent of your writing time. A better idea is to immediately decide your position and begin writing as soon as possible. (As you write, you might get better ideas for your essay.)

 RULE OF THUMB. Spend at most five minutes planning your essay and at least two minutes checking your essay for writing mistakes after you finish it. And never erase large blocks of text; that drains time and effort.

3. Take a strong position on the issue. Whenever you're asked to present your opinion or perspective on a topic, you have three choices: to agree, to disagree, or to draw a distinction. For example, if asked (on the SAT) whether it's better to make snap judgments instead of reasoned decisions, you can answer either yes it is, or no it isn't, or you can draw a distinction—that is, explain that your position depends on certain circumstances. Always be sure to state what your opinion depends on (if you're choosing the third option); never waffle on the issue by stating something inane such as "Sometimes it's better to make snap judgments, but at other times it's not."

Since the ACT topics are not in the form of yes/no questions, you cannot simply agree or disagree with them; however, you can look to the three given perspectives for guidance on developing your own opinion. It's best if you can clearly explain the relationship between your opinion and the three that are given. For example, you could say, "Perspective One makes an important point in stating that personal freedom can overshadow societal good, but I believe it exaggerates the consequences of increased freedom in our society."

4. Attend to the "ends." The opening and closing paragraphs are the main times your readers will ask themselves, "What score should this essay receive?" Therefore, make sure your introduction and conclusion are clear and well written; this will make it easier for your reader to understand the main points of your essay and reward it with a high score.

5-STAR TIP. It's best to start your essay with a thesis, a simple statement of your position. Don't spend too much space setting up the issue, establishing introductory examples, or (horror of horrors) quoting the prompt.

---

5. Make sure your examples support your thesis. Most of your essay should consist of concrete examples that are linked to and that prove your point (this is more important on the pre-2016 SAT, and less important on the ACT). These examples can be personal experiences, things you've read or heard about, historical or current events, or hypothetical scenarios. You should avoid choosing examples that generally relate to the topic but that do not directly back up your thesis.

BEST-KEPT SECRET. Generally, it's better to choose one or two more convincing examples than to present a laundry list of three or more simpler, less focused ones.

 EPIC FAIL! Don't turn your essay into a book report. If you decide to use Romeo and Juliet to prove your point about the power of love, you shouldn't go into details of the politics of Verona. (A short statement that "the two families were opposed" is more than enough.)

6. Make sure your essay flows well. Your readers will look for a logical direction to your essay: each sentence and paragraph should logically relate to both the previous and the next paragraph or sentence. When you're bringing up an entirely new point, you should try to tie the points together with a transition. There shouldn't be sentences that fall out of order, and your readers shouldn't have to stop and think, "How did this person get from this sentence to that?"

 5-STAR TIP. Try to use certain logical connectives (*therefore, then, although, moreover, in addition, in fact, on the other hand, by contrast, and so on*) that can connect two smaller ideas. It's even better if you can connect two larger points with a transitional sentence. This sentence might address similarities or differences between two examples or might show how the second point enhances or reinforces the first.

7. Develop your points fully—and deeply. It's important that you not dogmatically state a point such as "The Internet can be a distraction." Instead, you need to make that point deeper by adding an interesting example that supports the point, stating why that point is important or explaining when and why it is true. You also should use chains of reasoning to fully explain the point and connect it to the thesis (and, on the ACT, to the given perspectives). One such chain of reasoning would be, "Much of the content on the Internet is expressly designed to grab the viewer, making the Internet an ideal distraction. In fact, the Internet can be a distraction to itself, as when a viewer stops reading an article to check Facebook."

8. Strive to persuade the reader. Often the difference between the essays that earn the top score and those that earn the next-to-top score is that the better essays are more convincing. So when you write your essay, ask yourself, "Would anyone really believe this point based on what I've argued?" If the answer is no, try to develop your point to make it more convincing.

9. Address counterarguments, if appropriate. Counterarguments are points that support the opposite of your thesis. A counterargument to "We should always make reasoned decisions" is "Sometimes we don't have the time to weigh all the pros and cons." One way to be more persuasive is to defend your argument against these attacks by pointing out weaknesses in the counterargument. Sometimes this response will take up a whole paragraph, but you can often address a counterargument in just one or two sentences.

10. Pay attention to how it's written. Although your argument is the most important part of your essay, your readers will also be evaluating your writing skills. Here's some writing advice:

●*Use precise, but not showy, words*. Using more advanced vocabulary words is usually good, but misusing a big word can really hurt your work. For example, it's more exact to use "haughty" instead of "mean" to describe a person, but calling that same person "supercilious" doesn't make your essay better.

●*Vary your sentence structure*. Having many sentences that are about the same length is bad. Having many sentences that have the same grammatical construction is bad. Having many sentences that start or end with the same words is bad. Get it?

●*Make sure your essay is divided into paragraphs*. Each major point you make should be in a separate paragraph, and the introduction and conclusion should make up their own paragraphs. This helps the readers process your essay and shows knowledge of writing.

●*Avoid distracting grammatical errors*. Your readers are instructed not to count off for grammar mistakes but rather to factor them into the final score. The more distracted readers are by an error, the more tempted they'll be to dock points because of it. So spelling "rendezvous" as "rendesvous" is not a big deal, but omitting a word or spelling "whether" as "weather," can be more serious. To catch most of these errors, proofread your essay once you're finished writing.

BONUS TIP. On the ACT, make sure to label the perspectives given in the prompt with appropriate numbers when referring to them. When the readers see these numbers, it'll be easier for them to see that you've engaged the perspectives.

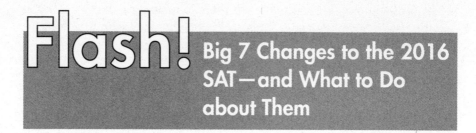

Flash! Big 7 Changes to the 2016 SAT—and What to Do about Them

You might have heard that there are changes coming to the SAT in March 2016. Well, you'd be right—but it's hard to figure out the true effects of changes labeled "Relevant Words in Context" and "The Great Global Conversation and US Founding Documents." (Not to keep you in suspense, these basically mean "fewer obscure words" and "a few more politically motivated passages.") No worries, though. You'll be able to ace the new test if you understand the 7 top changes to the 2016 SAT—and what to do about them.

1. No guessing penalty

The change: On the pre-2016 SAT, you lost a quarter point for each incorrect answer so that random guessing earns no more points than leaving every answer blank. The SAT has decided to do away with this penalty, eliminating the downside to guessing.

What to do: Always, always, always guess. This holds true even on the pre-2016 SAT and therefore especially applies to the new SAT.

2. No more sentence-completion questions

The change: The pre-2016 SAT contained fill-in-the-blank sentence completion questions that tested knowledge of obscure vocabulary. These questions have been eliminated; in their place will be questions assessing knowledge of vocabulary in a passage.

What to do: Put down the list of 500 SAT words and pick up some practice tests. Study the questions that are worded like "As used in line 30, 'excite' most nearly means what?"

EXTRA POINTER. For more on these passage-based vocabulary questions, see tip 8 in "Top 10 Strategies for the Reading Section."

REALITY CHECK. Other than the lack of sentence completions, the reading section won't change very much from the old SAT to the new one.

ON THE WEB. For more on the 2016 SAT's reading section, see HTTPS://COLLEGEREADINESS.COLLEGEBOARD.ORG/SAT-SUITE-ASSESSMENTS/PRACTICE/READING.

3. A completely passage-based writing section

The change: The 2016 SAT eliminates the Improving Sentences and Identifying Sentence Errors portions of the writing section. The resulting Writing and Language section looks very much like the ACT's English section today: one long passage with questions that ask you how best to revise, insert, or delete portions of text.

What to do: Get familiar with this new section by trying out some practice questions, both from the new SAT and from the current ACT.

ON THE WEB. For more on the 2016 SAT's Writing and Language section, see HTTPS://COLLEGEREADINESS.COLLEGEBOARD .ORG/SAT-SUITE-ASSESSMENTS/PRACTICE/WRITING-LANGUAGE.

EXTRA POINTER. More information on how the old SAT, new SAT, and ACT formats compare, as well as some tips for all formats, can be found in "Top 10 Tips for the English Section."

4. A large focus on "quantitative literacy" throughout the entire test

The change: All three sections of the 2016 SAT will contain some questions that require analyzing numerical data. On the reading and writing sections, a few questions will ask you to interpret provided graphs and charts. (No computation is required for these questions.) On the math section, the beefed-up Problem Solving and Data Analysis subsection will focus on some concepts that would not be out of place in a first-year statistics class.

What to do: Develop your skills in reading charts, graphs, and tables by studying current ACT science questions and new SAT math questions.

5-STAR TIP. If you have some time before taking the SAT, consider taking a statistics class if your school offers it. It will make the SAT statistics problems much easier and you'll learn some math that's useful for many data-centric fields. (You may be getting statistics as part of one of your algebra courses—check it out.)

5. An emphasis on different types of math

The change: On the new SAT, you'll see many fewer geometry problems and many more algebra problems, especially ones that ask you to solve equations. There will also be more statistics (as per the previous tip) and, for the first time on the SAT, relatively intricate trigonometry.

What to do: Make sure you've taken the right math courses (two algebra courses, one geometry course, and one trigonometry course). In addition, get really good at solving and manipulating equations: linear equations, quadratic equations, exponential equations, rational equations, systems of equations, and equations of circles. (Ask your math teacher or a brainy friend if you're not familiar with all of these.)

EXTRA POINTER. You'll also notice more rate problems on the new SAT math section. You know the ones: they ask you about miles per gallon, meters per second, and cookies sold per day. To solve these, consider using the method of dimensional analysis (again, ask your math teacher or brainy friend if you're drawing a blank).

ON THE WEB. For more information about the 2016 SAT math section in general, see HTTPS://COLLEGEREADINESS.COLLEGEBOARD .ORG/SAT-SUITE-ASSESSMENTS/PRACTICE/MATH.

For more information on the four subsections of the new SAT math section, check out the following links:

HTTPS://COLLEGEREADINESS.COLLEGEBOARD.ORG/SAT-SUITE-ASSESSMENTS/PRACTICE/MATH/HEART-OF-ALGEBRA

HTTPS://COLLEGEREADINESS.COLLEGEBOARD.ORG/SAT-SUITE-ASSESSMENTS/PRACTICE/MATH/PROBLEM-SOLVING-DATA-ANALYSIS

HTTPS://COLLEGEREADINESS.COLLEGEBOARD.ORG/SAT-SUITE-ASSESSMENTS/PRACTICE/MATH/ADVANCED-MATH

6. A noncalculator math section.

The change: On the pre-2016 SAT, a calculator is permitted (but not required) for each question. On the 2016 SAT, at least one math section will not allow the use of a calculator.

What to do: Brush up on the by-hand methods of adding, subtracting, multiplying, and dividing and get used to manipulating equations by hand.

7. A new (optional) analytical essay.

The change: Instead of the old "give your opinion on an issue" essay prompt, the 2016 SAT essay gives you a persuasive passage (much like ones you see on the reading section) and asks you to read the passage and explain how it builds an argument with evidence, reasoning, and stylistic and persuasive techniques. You'll have twice as much time as on the pre-2016 SAT (50 minutes, up from 25). You'll be assessed on *Reading* (how well did you understand the passage and provide textual evidence to support your claims?); *Analysis* (how well did you answer the question and explain how each technique builds the author's argument?), and *Writing* (how good is your thesis, introduction, conclusion, word choice, sentence structure, and grammar?).

What to do: For the new essay, keep your focus on explaining the argument, not simply summarizing the passage. Elaborate all your points and make sure to explain why and how a technique you identify (such as appeal to authority) helps build the argument. And if you can't adapt to the new essay, consider not taking it—the essay is optional, after all (unless the college you're considering requires it).

 ON THE WEB. For more information about the 2016 SAT essay section, see HTTPS://COLLEGEREADINESS.COLLEGEBOARD.ORG/SAT-SUITE-ASSESSMENTS/PRACTICE/ESSAY.

The essay's scoring rubric (well worth a look) can be found at HTTPS://COLLEGEREADINESS.COLLEGEBOARD.ORG/SAT-SUITE-ASSESSMENTS/PRACTICE/ESSAY/SCORING.

ON THE WEB. The best strategy for adapting to the new SAT is practice. You can find sample questions, including sample essay answers, at HTTPS://COLLEGEREADINESS.COLLEGEBOARD.ORG/SAMPLE-QUESTIONS.

Free, full practice tests for the 2016 SAT are at HTTPS://COLLEGEREADINESS.COLLEGEBOARD.ORG/SAT-SUITE-ASSESSMENTS/PRACTICE/PRACTICE-TESTS.

The general site for the 2016 SAT is HTTPS://COLLEGEREADINESS.COLLEGEBOARD.ORG/. You'll find even more information, as well as links to Khan Academy practice material, there.

 BONUS TIP. One easy way to get into the new SAT is to take the new PSAT first. Both will change formats in the 2015–2016 school year (the PSAT in October 2015, the SAT in March 2016), and the PSAT will provide the best practice for the new SAT.

FLASH! For an interesting article on how colleges will treat the 2016 SAT (Will they accept both pre-2016 and 2016 versions? Will the writing section be required? Will they superscore?), check out:

WWW.APPLEROUTH.COM/BLOG/2015/02/16/HOW-WILL-TOP-COLLEGES-USE-THE-REDESIGNED-SAT/.

And for an unusually detailed comparison of all the standardized tests, old and new, PSAT, SAT, and ACT, have a look at:

WWW.COMPASSPREP.COM/WP-CONTENT/UPLOADS/2014/12/REDESIGNED-SAT-SPEC-SHEET.PDF.

5 CONSTRUCTING THE APPLICATIONS

Needless to say, you won't be able to get into college if you don't apply. Now you could view your applications as a dreaded task in which you have to face up to all sorts of shortfalls in your accomplishments and achievements. But that's no way to look at it. Instead, think of it as the time when you get to present yourself in your very best light and strut your stuff. You're not trying to be someone else or pretend that you've done stuff you haven't done. You're showcasing what you do have, while still being you.

It's very important that you make the effort to be sure that each piece of the application is polished up to a nice, shiny finish; you want each and every part of the application to present you in the best possible light. That's because colleges really do look at all the parts—or as they would put it, they judge your application holistically—and each part has its own distinct part to play in the whole. Don't be shy. And don't run out of steam and blow off parts of your application because it seems like too much trouble to carefully complete each part—or because you just want to get it over with. This chapter will make the actual process of *constructing* your application—that is, assembling the pieces to form a coherent whole—a lot easier. We'll tell you the

- ▶ Top 10 strategies for making your final list

- ▶ 9 things admission officers look for in an application

- ▶ Top 10 tips for writing the Common App essay

▶ 10 best ideas for filling out the activities section of the Common App

▶ Top 10 tips for getting awesome letters of recommendation

▶ 8 secrets for answering the supplemental questions

Top 10 Strategies for Making Your Final List

There comes a time when you have to make a final list of colleges to apply to, and, for many students, there are still a million unresolved questions: How many schools should I apply to? What balance should there be among reach schools, reasonable bets, and safety schools? How much should I consider the finances? How much say should my counselor and parents have in making the list? Should I pick a broad variety of kinds of schools or would it be good to narrow the focus? Should I be applying early decision or early action? There's no one answer to these and related questions—no one size fits all—and, yet, you'll have an easier time if you follow our ten best tips for narrowing down the choices to a final list.

1. Review the data. By the time it comes to making your final list of colleges you're going to apply to, you might have been researching colleges for a year or even more. And you might have attended a dozen or more college rep visits and college fairs, visited ten or more college campuses, reviewed dozens of glossy brochures and countless more college web pages, and even talked to a slew of current attendees or recent graduates of the colleges you're considering. So now's the time to assemble the data—here's where your college notebook (either physical or virtual) comes in handy—and fill in any remaining gaps (either because you can't remember the information or because you never had it in the first place). An informed decision requires proper, organized information.

2. Weigh the alternatives. Now's the time you'll have to make the decision about which colleges will—and will not—make the cut. Some colleges you initially thought you might be interested in can be eliminated right away: either because you saw something on your campus visit that really turned you off, or because you found out that pigs would fly before you could get into that school, or because it turned out that even with the best financial aid package you could hope for it would be way beyond your budget. But many schools will still be in the running (if you've made a good initial list).

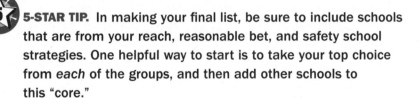

IOHO. Rather than making a score sheet, in which you assign a percentage to each of a number of different factors then try to score each of the contenders on each of the metrics, we advise you to consider the colleges holistically (which is the way colleges consider you). Try to assess how much you like each college, all things considered: the academics and program, the social and residential life, the location and distance from home, and so on. It's not necessary that you come up with a ranking, just a list of colleges, any one of which would be desirable given your abilities, personality, and goals.

5-STAR TIP. In making your final list, be sure to include schools that are from your reach, reasonable bet, and safety school strategies. One helpful way to start is to take your top choice from *each* of the groups, and then add other schools to this "core."

3. Find your focus. While at the beginning of the selection process you might have cast your net widely, now is the time to narrow down the list to colleges that have a common nature: could be a college of a certain type (four-year private college, state university, small liberal arts college, engineering school, community college, etc.); of a certain size (less than 2,500 students, 2,500 to 7,500, 7,500 to 15,000, 15,000 to 30,000, or more than 30,000); in a certain location (north or south, east or west, near home or far away); or any combination of those factors.

 EXTRA POINTER. Play to your advantages. If you have some talent or skill that makes it more likely that you'll get into some sort of school, be sure to apply to a good sampling of that kind of school. For example, if you have real distinction in sports or the arts or you have an especially strong background in science, math, or engineering, be sure to apply to enough schools that are looking for students with those credentials. And, if one or both of your parents went to a particular college, by all means include those colleges in your list (provided they meet your focus). Many colleges give preference to so-called "legacy" applicants, and there's no reason not to up your chances by applying to one of these schools.

4. Don't make your list into a Chinese restaurant menu.
Some students (and their families) approach making the list in the way they would order from an old-fashioned Chinese restaurant menu: one from column A, one from column B, and one from column C. That is, they put two or three colleges on the list, their parents add another two or three choices, and maybe their high school counselor contributes three or four entries. This is an extremely bad and high-risk strategy. Not only do you lose any focus, but, in the worst case, you get into only two or three colleges—and none of them is among the ones *you* picked!

Instead of compromising in this way, by giving everyone their say, integrate your choices: discuss with all the participants what matters to you in a college, then strive to reach agreement about which colleges satisfy those parameters. Often a counselor—and, yes, even a parent—can reach agreement with you, once he or she understands clearly what you meant.

REALITY CHECK. If you do have family conflicts about which—and what kinds of—schools you are to apply to, it's very important that they be resolved at this stage. If your parents are adamant about your going to college in-state, but you're eager to run for the hills, it's important that you reach some sort of agreement at this point. It'll be three times as hard to reach agreement once you've actually gotten in to two or three in-state colleges.

5. Figure out the finances. As with buying any product, it's good to have a price range in mind once you start seriously shopping—and applying is seriously shopping. Use the net price calculator for each of the colleges you're thinking of putting on your list to see whether the projected price falls within your budget. Keep in mind, though, that *merit* aid is not included in the results, so if you're applying to schools that offer merit aid, and if you stand out as a really good applicant for the school in question, the total price might be much less that the tool indicates. Also, keep in mind that, especially if you get good admits, you might be able to get a school to match a competing offer, thereby bringing the price lower than the tool predicts. (For more on this, see our "Top 10 Tips for Assessing the Financial Aid Offer," at the end of Chapter 6.)

 ON THE WEB. For a list of colleges that completely meet financial need (at least according to their calculations), check out WWW.USNEWS.COM/EDUCATION/BEST-COLLEGES/PAYING-FOR-COLLEGE/ARTICLES/2014/09/15/COLLEGES-AND-UNIVERSITIES-THAT-CLAIM-TO-MEET-FULL-FINANCIAL-NEED.

 REALITY CHECK. Finances is another area where there could be family conflict, so be sure to run the numbers by whoever the payer might be: parents, grandparents, or whoever. And, if the estimated package includes student loans, make sure you've thought about whether you are really willing to take on that amount of debt in exchange for a college degree from that school.

6. Don't apply scoreless. You might be amazed to hear this, but some students apply to college without having taken the ACT or SAT—or having taken it, but planning to take it again, and planning (for whatever reason) to get a better score. You need to know where you stand standard-test-wise to make a reasonable choice of what schools to apply to, so work only with the scores you have.

EXTRA POINTER. If you're thinking of applying Early Decision or Early Action Single Choice, be sure you understand at this point exactly what the rules are—and what you are (and are not) committing yourself to. Each school has somewhat different rules about where else to apply to and whether you're committed to go if they take you, and it'd be shame if you unwittingly eliminated other choices that would have been better for you, financially, academically, or socially. For more on the early's, see "Applying Early? 10 Questions to Ask If You're Considering Early Decision or Early Action," in chapter 2.

---

7. Follow a bell curve. Though different advisors have different opinions—and different students have different risk tolerances—we think that in choosing schools to apply to you should follow a bell curve: 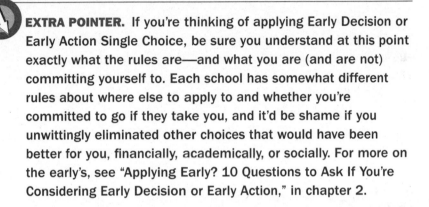 a few schools that are long shots (also known as "reach" schools), many schools that are good or at least reasonable bets, and a few schools that are sure things (a.k.a. "safeties"). Use objective measures, such as your SAT/ACT scores (in conjunction with each school's 25 to 75 percent band of admits), GPA, and class rank (if your school has that) to assess your chances.

IOHO. Apply to reach schools only if you're emotionally prepared for the disappointment that comes with being turned down. The reason it's a reach is that it's unlikely you'll get in. If getting rejected is going to color the rest of your application process, spare yourself the grief.

---

8. Realize that middle of the range doesn't mean good bet. One of the main things you should consider in narrowing down your list is the 25 to 75 percent band: this tells you where the middle half of the class (25 to 75 percent of admits) fell on the SAT or ACT range. But keep in mind that hitting the band isn't a guarantee of admissions, and, for some, doesn't even indicate good chances. If you come in at the 25 percent point (and if no other factors were considered in the admissions decision) the chances would be stacked 3 to 1 against you. Not such good odds.

9. Pick safe bets that you could imagine yourself going to. One key thing to keep in mind is that in picking sure bets you should pick schools that you would actually feel comfortable going to if they were the only colleges you got into. You never know with 100 percent certainty how the application process will end up, and there are plenty of easy-to-get-into schools that you can consider.

 RULE OF THUMB. If you fall on the 75th percentile or better on the 25 to 75 percent ACT/SAT band or if the school accepts more than 70 percent of applicants, then it's probably a reasonably safe bet, except at the most elite schools where they have many, many overqualified students to choose from. Of course, schools that have open admissions, where you are guaranteed a place if you have taken at least the required minimum high school program, are a sure bet.

---

10. Don't apply to crazy many schools. Some students think it a badge of honor to apply to many, many, many colleges. Fifteen, twenty, even (we've heard) thirty: the more you apply, the better your chances. But it isn't necessarily true. For one thing, as you no doubt know already, it can be a lot of work to prepare even a single good application (especially ones that have supplemental questions and/or essays) and having too many to complete can dilute the quality of each. For another thing, shoveling in dozens of applications in some cases is functioning as a way of putting off making decisions about even what kind of school you want to go to—unhealthy procrastination. And finally, choosing to submit so many applications can be an incredible extra expense at seventy-five dollars a pop, and, worse yet, an expression of groundless anxiety—not a healthy thing.

 RULE OF THUMB. Don't apply to more colleges than you have fingers (or maybe, fingers and a couple of toes).

 ON THE WEB. To find out how much different colleges cost to apply to, check out WWW.USNEWS.COM/EDUCATION/BEST-COLLEGES/ THE-SHORT-LIST-COLLEGE/ARTICLES/2014/09/16/COLLEGES-THAT-CHARGE-THE-MOST-FOR-APPLYINGN. Or just go the admissions page of each of the colleges' websites.

 ON THE WEB. Trying to decide how many to apply to? You might enjoy WWW.NYTIMES.COM/2014/11/16/NYREGION/APPLICATIONS-BY-THE-DOZEN-AS-ANXIOUS-STUDENTS-HEDGE-COLLEGE-BETS.HTML?_R=1.

9 Things Admission Officers Look for in an Application

If you've been to a college night or college fair, or if you've participated in an information session on a college visit, you've probably heard some fearless student or parent asking, "So what do I (or my son or daughter) need to get into your school?" And the admissions officer or regional representative answers, "There's no minimum score or grade point, because we evaluate *holistically*." But, really. There *is* a set of features that differentiates some applications from others, that makes some applicants rise up out of the stack. Here are nine of the most important things readers look for in an application.

1. Good objective scores. You won't be surprised to hear that at many of the more selective schools, the quantitative data—your SAT or ACT scores, your GPA and class standing, the number of AP courses you took and how you did, and perhaps your SAT II and state tests—loom large. That's because these scores provide a quick and dirty way of establishing levels of students. And, though virtually no school will tell you what the cutoff score is for admission to their school (if even there is one), they do provide a range of scores that last year's class had, the so-called 25 to75 percent band. Why would they do that if scores weren't very important?

2. Students who challenge themselves. Whether it's taking a rigorous course load, being the main agent of an activity, creating a new club or pushing oneself in a tough sport, admissions officers respond to students who reach beyond the bounds of what's easy. It can be out-of-class or out-of-state, but finding ways to engage that go beyond the ordinary can distinguish an application. One thing to think about is the depth of your commitment and the ways you effectuate it. Some students might take especially challenging courses at their high school or even on the web or at a local college. Some students might seek out summer internships or work opportunities to develop a skill, interest, or passion. Some students might undertake very extensive community service and develop high-impact programs over a number of years. Whatever you do that goes beyond the norm can signal to colleges that you will also be motivated to go beyond the norm when you're accepted to their college.

3. Good communication skills. One of the things admissions officers are on the lookout for is a good ability to express oneself. This is why colleges ask for a writing sample and often read very carefully the samples they do receive—whether the Common App essays, supplemental questions each college itself might ask, or the writing section of the ACT or essay of the SAT (this is why surprisingly many schools require the standardized tests "with writing"). For this reason, in composing your essays on your application you should pay special attention not only to answering the exact questions asked but also to writing in a way that is natural, careful, and well argued. Also, in case you have an oral interview or discussion with an alumnus, campus rep, or other person from the college, you should carefully answer his or her questions in an informed and responsive way (see our pieces "Top 10 Tips for Writing the Common App Essay" and "Top 12 Tips for Nailing the On- (or Off-) Campus Interview," respectively, for more on writing the essay and being interviewed.)

4. Knowledge of their institution. One of the things admissions officers are most interested in finding out about you is how seriously you are considering their college and how well you would fit in, if accepted. And one of the main ways they have of finding out these things is to see how you respond when asked hidden—and not-so-hidden—questions about why you want to go to their college.

Specificity is king. When asked on a supplemental question something about yourself or their institution or both, be sure to offer some reason for picking their school that does not apply to every other school and that was not the single thing they said five times at the college rep visit, college night, or information session—for example, that their school has an open curriculum, that their school has a design-your-own-major program, or that their school was grade-free for the first year. They know all those things (and, in case they forgot, countless other applicants recount them for them). Instead, find something *particular and specific* that makes you want to go to their school—for example, a special program or major, something about the goals or values of that school, or some career path for which the school trains you especially well. Every college wants to feel special and, more important, that you've taken the time to figure out why it's special.

 5-STAR TIP. Some colleges are more interested in intrinsic rather than instrumental reasons for your wanting to go to their college. That is, your burning desire to study microbiology (combined with their school's excellence in that field) is more impressive to them than your desire to use that college as a stepping-stone to med school. Think the next four years in presenting yourself, as well as the next ten.

EXTRA POINTER. In preparing for an interview, either on- or off- campus, make sure you prepare material tailored to each interviewer. He or she would also like to feel his institution is special—and that you've taken the trouble to find out why.

---

5. Intellectual vitality. Defining this characteristic is tricky, but admissions officers cite it constantly. If a spark of the bright mind comes out in your essays, if your activities seem to suggest that you are looking for academic adventures, or your recommendations speak of your eager and creative contributions to the classroom, these all hint at intellectual lift. Do you seem like someone who would add life to a study group or be a great lab partner? Do you appear to enjoy conversations of substance? Much of college is spent in those environments, so admissions folks are on the hunt for students who demonstrate this hard-to-define, but I-know-it-when-I-see-it character trait.

6. Emotional maturity. Making good choices, taking personal responsibility, having a goal in your life and having some idea how to achieve it—all of these are signs of your emotional maturity: that you're thinking and acting more like a college student than a high school student. The admissions officer is trying to imagine how you'll fit into their first-year class (and beyond). Help them out by showing your (soon-to-be-in) college side.

7. Contributions to your community. One of the things you hear admissions officers talking most about is "building" or "sculpting" a class, by which they mean that not only do they want to pick students who they think will succeed academically but also students who will bring a broad variety of skills, interests, and talents to their college community. The main way they have of gauging what you might bring to the community is by seeing what communal experiences you have had in your home community—both high school and the city or town beyond.

Be sure to highlight in your list of extracurricular activities any activities that point beyond yourself to your high school at-large: managing the talent show or coordinating the Bible study group, for example, both involve significant other-directed activity. And any outreach or service projects in your city, town, or place of worship can help establish that at college, too, you'll play a role in their community (rather than being holed up in the library 24/7). If, for example, you've worked in a soup kitchen, or helped build houses for poor families, or worked to clean up a town after a tornado, be sure to showcase your contributions.

8. Recommendations that sing. Teacher recommendations address many desirable characteristics, including academic promise, willingness to accept challenge, intellectual vitality, writing skills, and many others. Accordingly, you should seek out recommenders who know you well and from classes where you were successful (also, if you showed marked growth or improvement in some course, this should be considered, too). Chances are those teachers will sing your praises and help to build the background characteristics we've listed that will add to the strength of your application. (For more details on how to get the best letters of recommendation see "Top 10 Tips for Getting Awesome Letters of Recommendation" later in this chapter)

9. True distinction. It doesn't happen often, but once in a while a student really stands above the crowd in some pursuit. Some students are accomplished musicians, some have distinguished themselves in state or national math or science competitions, some have won writing prizes or have had material published, some have achieved great feats in one or another sport. If you're lucky enough to be one of these, make sure your accomplishment rises in high relief in your application: a mention in your personal essay or answer to some question, something you highlight and develop in an interview, or something you ask a teacher or high school counselor to incorporate into their letter. Whatever the case, make sure that the reader (who might have a stack of 100 applications to slog his or her way through) notices your special distinction. Don't be overly modest here.

REALITY CHECK. If you're applying for admission to an ultra-selective national university, you'll have your best shot if one or other of your achievements has national standing. If you have one such achievement, make sure it is prominently put forth in your application.

BONUS TIP. You're not going to believe this, but some universities tell you on their website what they're looking for at their school. Do a Google search for *what [name of university] looks for*, and see what comes up. Then tailor your application accordingly. For two especially detailed and candid examples, see HTTP://ADMISSIONS.CORNELL.EDU/APPLY/WHAT-CORNELL-LOOKS and HTTPS://COLLEGE.HARVARD.EDU/ADMISSIONS/APPLICATION-PROCESS/WHAT-WE-LOOK

Top 10 Tips for Writing the Common App Essay

What follows is the Common App's latest report on what most students find the most challenging part of the college-application process: the dreaded personal essay.

2015–2016 COMMON APPLICATION ESSAY PROMPTS. We are pleased to share the 2015–2016 Essay Prompts with you. New language appears in italics:

1. *Some students have a background, identity, interest, or talent that is so meaningful they believe their application would be incomplete without it.* If this sounds like you, then please share your story.

2. *The lessons we take from failure can be fundamental to later success.* Recount an incident or time when you experienced failure. How did it affect you, and what did you learn from the experience?

3. Reflect on a time when you challenged a belief or idea. What prompted you to act? Would you make the same decision again?

4. *Describe a problem you've solved or a problem you'd like to solve. It can be an intellectual challenge, a research query, an ethical dilemma—anything that is of personal importance, no matter the scale. Explain its significance to you and what steps you took or could be taken to identify a solution.*

5. Discuss an accomplishment or event, formal or informal, that marked your transition from childhood to adulthood within your culture, community, or family.

The changes you see reflect the feedback and consensus of nearly 6,000 individuals who responded to our recent survey....

In the Common App essay, you're asked to tell something personal about yourself that will somehow help the admissions officer distinguish you from the hordes of other applicants whose admissions folders are still stacked up in front of him or her. All in the space of two or three pages. Sound daunting? Wouldn't have to be. Especially after you've benefitted from our 10 best tips for attacking the Common App essay prompt:

1. Allow yourself enough time. As opposed to other parts of the Common App, which if you're organized can be polished off in a reasonably short amount of time, the essay prompt is, in every case, time-consuming. That's because, first, it's hard to reflect on yourself (most of us spent most time *being* ourselves, not thinking about what it's like to be ourselves); second, it's hard to select a single event, aspect of one's personality, or accomplishment that is representative of one's self (most of us are complexes of many occurrences, traits, and dimensions); and, third, it's hard to distill and refine this feature into an essay that's communicative to another person (most of us find it hard to talk about ourselves in a way that makes sense to other people). So, start work on your personal essay early. You'll need lots of time to write and rewrite, to add and subtract, to show to others and incorporate their comments and suggestions, and, most important, to write an essay that you yourself are satisfied with.

IOHO. It's a good idea to tackle the personal essay before turning to the other parts of the Common App (once you've finished the hardest part, the other parts will seem much easier) and to begin work on the personal essay the summer before the beginning of your senior year (that way, you'll have plenty of time for your ideas to jell, change, and calcify).

2. Consider all the choices and what it would take to answer each. Many students look over the questions and immediately lunge at one: "experienced failure? —I can think of a couple of times right off the bat"; "challenged a belief?—sure, I just did that just last month." But it's important that you think about all the choices before fixating on one (you might try sketching out for yourself answers to each of the questions before even tentatively selecting one). For one thing, you might be able to come up with a more interesting, revealing, or moving answer to a question other than the one you first selected. Or you might discover that you don't have enough things to say on a particular question (you're being asked to write about 650 words).

In making your choice, be sure to notice that some questions include more than one question. For example, in question 2, "Recount an incident or time when you experienced failure. How did it affect you, and what lessons did you learn from the experience?," you are being asked not just to recount the failure ("recount an incident or time when you experienced failure"), but also how you reacted to it ("how did it affect you") and what you took away from the incident ("and what did you learn from the experience?"). Similarly, in question 3, they ask you not only for a time you challenged a belief ("Reflect on a time when you challenged a belief or idea") but also what made you act ("What prompted you to act") and whether if you had it to do again you would have done the same thing ("Would you make the same decision again?"). Upshot? Think about how you'd answer all parts of the question before picking it—and make sure when you do answer it, you address each question in some detail.

 EPIC FAIL! As much as the Common App talks about an essay *prompt* (which might suggest to you free association, dumping of everything you know about the subject), what you're really being asked to produce is a carefully focused, well-developed answer to a question (or series of questions). If you're viewing the question as a springboard to say whatever you want, you're probably viewing it wrong.

5-STAR TIP. In many of these questions there's a single word whose meaning is important to your answering the question head-on. Be sure you know, for instance, exactly what *identity* means (question 1), a *belief or idea* is (question 3), what an *ethical dilemma* is (question 4), or what it is to *mark a transition* (question 5) before taking a stab at these questions. One of the easiest ways for a personal essay to go off the rails is by your not understanding the nuances of the terms being used to ask the question.

3. Pick the topic (and its content) yourself. Once you've honed in on the question to work on, the most natural thing to do is to ask around for suggestions about what to write about. Your parents, friends, high school counselor, college-attending brother or sister—all of these can seem like good sources for ideas on which question to pick and what to say. But be careful. The story you are going to have to tell is going to have to be your story—and one you are going to have to tell from the inside—so others could very well put you on a path that doesn't lead to a good essay. They are not you and can't give your perspective on things. Much better idea? You pick, develop, and refine your ideas—and then try them out on others (see tip 10 for more on this).

4. Turn inward. Virtually all of the other parts of the application ask about publicly available, objective facts: your ACT or SAT scores, your class rank, your extracurricular activities, and, perhaps, what you want to study at college. The personal essay, on the other hand, asks you to talk about what it's like being you—and how you feel about being you. Notice the very words in which the questions are posed: "a background, *identity*, interest, or talent ... so meaningful that [your] application would be incomplete without it"; "an incident or time when you *experienced* failure"; "anything that is of *personal* importance, no matter the scale"; "an accomplishment or event ... that marked *your* transition from childhood to adulthood ..."

An essay that answers the question—that *really* answers the question—will reflect not just on the events, incidents, and occurrences that prompted your response but also on the emotional response you had to those experiences: what it was like *for you*. Being fully reflective—and expressing the first-person perspective that only you can have about yourself—will not only come off as authentic—true to yourself—but also will help communicate your uniqueness as a person to the admissions officer reading your essay. Which will help you get in.

REALITY CHECK. Some care should be exercised if you are planning to write about *extremely* personal psychological issues. There's a thin line between the healthy personal growth that can attend overcoming an eating disorder or a bout with depression and a confessional essay that leaves the admissions officer wondering about whether you could really function at his or her college.

5. Focus on a single event. A good essay answers the question by *sampling*—that is, by selecting a single event, occurrence, or character trait that sheds light on who you are as a person—and helps the admissions officer gauge whether you would be a good admit to his or her college. You're not being asked (nor would it be a good idea) to provide an intellectual, personal, or emotional autobiography or, worse, to provide a résumé or list of accomplishments (not only is that information available elsewhere on your application but also it doesn't answer the question asked). Notice that each of the questions asks you to select *one*: "*a* background, identity, interest, or talent," "*an* incident or time," "*a* problem you've solved," "*an* accomplishment or event" (*a/an* = one, in all cases). What they're looking for is a window into your soul or self—but through a single event, in every instance.

5-STAR TIP. Since the whole essay is going to be centered on one event or decision, think carefully about which event to pick. Be sure to try out different possibilities—and shift to another—if you discover that the essay isn't going well.

BEST-KEPT SECRET. Since the admissions officer is basically asking him- or herself two questions—What is this applicant like? and How will he or she fit into my college as a first-year student?—it's important that you not pick an episode too trite or too high-school-ish. Unless you have something really deep and unusual to say (and in certain cases you could), it's best not to write about your first big breakup (or your second or third), your challenge to your school's dress code, or why being on the debating team is central to your identity.

6. Consider a struggle—and its resolution. Some of the questions asked can be best approached by considering a struggle you might have had at some point in your life. Some dimension or aspect of your identity, some experience of failure, some challenge to a belief or idea, some transition to adulthood—all can be accompanied by doubt, confusion, conflict, worry, regret, and repeated changes of mind. All of these feelings—and what followed them—can be good to talk about in your essay. Not only will they round you out, and make you more interesting and distinctive as a person, they will help ensure that your essay is of adequate length. Also, keep in mind that you need not have arrived at a 100 percent resolution of your struggle or conflict. Indeed partial successes, somewhat murky decisions, and halting transitions in life can often come off as more "real" —and more reflective of the maturity they're looking for in a college student—than fully successful, life-altering, no-regrets events.

7. Be detailed—vivid and particular. The best essays enable the reader to form a picture of what's going on: they have a vivacity, a lifelike, easily imaginable scenario that makes the reader feel that he or she is actually there—witnessing not just the event as it's going on but also what's going on inside the narrator as he or she tells about the event. To achieve this effect, you'll want to tell the reader lots of details about the event and your reaction; you'll want to develop your thoughts over the course of the paragraphs of your essay; and you'll want to focus on special, unusual, or unique particularities of your life story.

8. Carefully consider both ends. You might not have thought of this, but the admissions officer has dozens of essays to read and is striving to make sure that one doesn't blend with the next. One of the ways he or she does this is by paying special, focused attention to the very first paragraph—indeed, even the first sentence—of your essay. As a result, you should begin your answer to the question in the very first sentence (forget about the five-paragraph high school essay with its long, and usually contentless, introduction). There is no one, right way to start: some good essays start with a dramatic moment, some start with a (hopefully not too trite) quote or anecdote, and some start with a simple, direct beginning of an answer to the question asked. Also, carefully consider your last paragraph. You don't want to introduce something new, but you also don't want to just boringly sum up what you've said. End with what you most want the admissions officer to remember about you.

9. Write the drafts and edit them critically. Since writing the essay is the single hardest part of the Common App (see tip 1), you won't be surprised to hear that you'll have to write a pretty good number of drafts to get the essay sounding right. After you've written your first draft, put it aside for a few days, then ask yourself the following questions:

✔ Have I answered the question (in all its parts) head-on?

✔ Does my essay offer interesting and insightful information about me as a person?

✔ Is there a clear direction to my essay and does each part (paragraph, sentence) add something to the narrative as a whole?

✔ Does my essay present me in a positive light and make the admissions officer want to admit me to the community that is his or her college?

After answering these questions, make the appropriate changes—taking something out, adding an example or illustration, rearranging the points, or whatever—to strengthen your essay. Then, edit your essay for these stylistic issues:

✔ Could some passive constructions be changed into active verbs?

✔ Are there more expressive adjectives you could substitute for more vague and colorless ones?

✔ Could some of your sentence constructions be changed or varied?

✔ Could more pretentious or awkward words be replaced by more ordinary and appropriate ones?

All of these seemingly simple and local changes can make for an essay that reads better and more convincingly, overall.

 EXTRA POINTER. Be sure to proofread your essay and to correct errors that your spell-checker misses: homonyms—*there, they're,* and *their; it's* and *its; to, too,* and *two; principal* and *principle;* transpositions (*run* and *urn, frat* and *fart*); truncations (*then* and *hen, mother* and *other*); wrong prepositions (*of, on,* and *or; an, in,* and *on*); missing or extra words (*the college I want apply to, the a person*).

10. Get feedback. Once you've written your near-final draft show your essay, together with the question it's answering, to two or three readers—a teacher or your high school counselor, for sure, and a few parents, friends, or college-attending siblings, in addition. Solicit from them suggestions about how the essay could be made better—and give their comments a serious consideration (rather than thinking, "I'm done with this essay, and besides, what do any of these people really know about college-application essays, anyway?"). But don't simply fold and throw out or significantly change your essay unless there is good reason to do so. Your readers are just giving their opinions, and, ultimately, it's your self to reflect on, your story to tell, and your essay to write.

ON THE WEB. For people who like this sort of thing, there's interesting information on why the Common App made the changes they did to the 2015–2016 edition. Go to HTTP://BLOG .COMMONAPP.ORG/2015/03/31/2015-2016-ESSAY-PROMPTS/ and see what they're thinking.

BONUS TIP. Though over five hundred schools participate in the Common App, including no doubt many of the ones you're applying to, some schools do not. You'll be happy to hear that the tips we've given on writing the Common App essay will work equally well for any essay. Just adapt the tips to the question(s) they're asking and your essay will stand out from the rest.

10 Best Ideas for Filling Out the Activities Section of the Common App

Seems like it'd be a snap. Take about half-an-hour, jot down a couple of extracurricular activities, and you're done. After all, you've got good grades and a pretty good ACT score, so what's it going to matter if you were lead singer in the A Capellas or president of the Service Ambassadors? But wait. Turns out that colleges do care about what you're doing when you're not glued to your seat in class or holed up in your room doing homework. That's because at many schools admissions officers are charged with building a community—a first-year class with a diverse set of interests and a broad range of abilities. Wanna join 'em? You'll stand the best shot if you follow our ten best tips for showcasing your extracurriculars.

1. Cast the net widely. You might have thought that extracurricular activities include only the traditional clubs and teams whose photos appear in the yearbook: you know, debating team, student government, band, cheer, chess club, and so on. But think more creatively—and expansively. Were you a member of any more unusual club at school: model UN, Mandarin Chinese lunch group, LGBTQ advocacy club, or the Random Acts of Kindness society? And how about activities outside of school? Were you a member of the Habitat for Humanity service group, the Community Vegetable Garden seed group, or the Conversation Partners for International Students? Finally, work experiences, summer internships, even family responsibilities can all count as extracurricular activities—especially if you did something distinctive or that in some important way contributed to your personal or intellectual growth.

2. Focus on the most recent. Colleges are most interested in who you are today (and will probably be next fall), so be sure to list only your current activities—that is, those that you've been doing in high school. The person reading your application won't be interested in the fact that you won the seventh-grade spelling bee.

5-STAR TIP. Be sure to check the "Do you plan to participate in college" box if there's any chance you might continue the activity in college (you don't need to be 100 percent certain, and there's no commitment here). Not only does this show your continuing interest in the activity in question—colleges like to see ongoing commitment to a particular pursuit—but also if the college actually has a club, team, or program in your area of interest, they'll feel you could become a member or fill a slot.

REALITY CHECK. Don't blithely check the box for every one of your extracurricular activities. No college admissions officer is going to believe that, in addition to your four or five first-year courses, you're going to do a dozen extracurricular activities.

3. List the most important first. It might strike you as natural to list your activities in chronological order (either ascending or descending). Don't. The extracurricular section isn't meant to be a year-by-year history of what you've done but rather a weighted list of what activities you think define you most as a person.

5-STAR TIP. If you have one super-showy extracurricular activity—say you spent a summer at an incredibly-hard-to-get-into math camp, or you redesigned the city's transportation map (and had your map selected), or you set up an ACT-prep club for homeless kids in your community—showcase it in the first position (and explain it in detail). The admissions officer might be quickly scanning each student's list (especially if he or she has dozens to read), and a real show-stopper right up front is guaranteed to catch his or her attention (and make him or her attend more carefully to the other entries on your list).

EXTRA POINTER. If an important activity doesn't fit neatly into the categories provided in the drop-down menu, no problem. Use the title "Other Club/Activity" at the end of the list but be sure in this case to provide as much explanation of the activity as space allows.

EPIC FAIL! Resist the temptation to throw in a humorous aside to your activity list like "Chilling with friends," "Hanging out ... " or "Watching HBO." Admission officers take their jobs very seriously and they react badly when you don't regard the application in the same way.

4. Use active, task-oriented language. The Activities section gives you very little space for each of your activities. Use it wisely. Begin with the name of the club, providing a brief explanation or gloss if it's not immediately clear what the club is or what it does (who knows what FISH is, what the Key Club does, or what MV Snow Burns is up to?). Then offer two or three tightly worded phrases, using past tense, strong verbs, to say what the group—and what *you*—did (e.g., "tutored eight math students, increased their grades by an average of nine points, sensitized me to the needs of struggling students; "founded" [rather than just "attended" or "was in"] the *Bulgaclub* in which we read five short stories and one novel by the Russian fantasy-writer, Mikhail Bulgakov").

EXTRA POINTER. If you're not sure how to get your achievement down to the space allotted—or if you don't have a good repertoire of action verbs—check out some of the descriptions at www.linkedin.com. Put in a common name and see how various space-pressed professionals showcase their achievements.

5. Emphasize leadership roles. One of the things colleges are most looking for in an application is the diffuse quality of leadership. Give them what they want. If you were captain of the quiz bowl team, student-body president, editor-in-chief of the yearbook, coordinator of the talent show, head tour guide for prospective students, lead cashier at the pharmacy, or even scheduler of deliveries at the florist—all of these count as leadership positions that colleges are interested in. If you were the founder, president, leader, manager, or concertmaster of some club or team, make sure you highlight that on your application.

EXTRA POINTER. You don't have to be the head honcho to be a leader: treasurers, assistant managers, advisors, and tutors are also properly considered leaders. Also there are some things to mention even if you weren't a "leader": did you plan an event, mediate a conflict, or help advertise a program? Colleges are interested in those, too.

---

6. Don't feel pressured to list ten. Just because the Common App gives you space for ten activities doesn't mean you should list ten. A few strong activities in which you've invested significant time and that show something important about your interests, goals, and values as an individual can easily trump a list of eight or nine half-baked activities. You want to come off as a focused and thoughtful individual, not a dabbler or dilettante.

REALITY CHECK. If your family circumstances have left you little time for traditional extracurricular activities, know that admissions officers understand and respect this reality (indeed, properly described, it can show not only leadership but character). Be honest and open if you've had to work your way through high school; care for a parent, sibling, or child; or suffered your own physical or emotional health issues.

---

7. Don't be flummoxed by the how-much-time questions. It may feel strange to fill out "hours spent per week" and "weeks spent per year" lines. But relax. All they're trying to gauge is the scope and depth of the activity: Was it a once-a-week club for a semester or two or did you spend ten hours a week throughout your high school career? Was it a week-long summer camp after your sophomore year or was it two summer-long internships combined with continuing part-time work throughout the school year? Answer the hours questions as honestly as you can but avoid puffing up (or tamping down) the data. There are only so many hours in the day and no one will believe you spent every out-of-school hour on extracurricular activities.

BEST-KEPT SECRET. In most cases, admissions officers think it better to have worked lots of hours, especially in both eleventh and twelfth grades, on a single project, or two or three, than to have flitted from project to project without any depth, direction, or commitment. So think carefully about how many hours you put down for the focal, or most important, activities. Within reason, more is better.

8. Don't be shy or self-effacing. Some students feel a little uncomfortable putting forward their activities or accomplishments: "What does it matter that I was president of the philosophy club; after all, it had only three members?" or "I'm not going to mention that I was class president, I hate standing out." But keep in mind that applying for college is a competitive activity, and, in all parts of the application, you should be putting yourself forward in the best light. So set aside your personal misgivings, apprehensions, and self-doubts and showcase your extracurricular activities as if it you mean it. Because you do.

9. Do a draft. Before entering any data online, collect all your activities, leadership positions, and accomplishments into a formatted list. Not only can you then cut and paste the data into the form, you can also play around with the wording and order for maximum effect (on the actual form you can only see the activities one-by-one, so it's hard to get a sense of how your presentation will strike the reader). And don't forget to do a spell-check; you wouldn't want colleges to discover you were the lead sexophone player in your school marching band.

EXTRA POINTER. If you've never made a résumé before, find out if your school uses Naviance, a very popular web-based software for high schools; the Family Connection section has a straightforward résumé builder feature you can use. Otherwise, do a simple web search for "résumé examples" or "résumé builder" and you'll find a wide range of free options for creating your own.

10. Keep it real. More than anything else, admissions officers are looking for an authentic and plausible picture of who you are and what you can bring to the college community. Lay it on too thick, and no one will believe you. Lay it on too thin and the college will think you have nothing to offer. Be true to your self—but to your best self.

FLASH! The Common Application activities section has what might strike one as a flaw. Overall, a green checkmark means you have completed the application, but the Activities section will show a green check without your having finished the section. Don't assume you're done when you see the green checkmark; instead, be sure to proof that section visually. Otherwise, you might accidentally send in your application with one activity—or none.

Top 10 Tips for Getting Awesome Letters of Recommendation

Colleges analyze a host of statistics in your application (SATs/ACTs, GPA, class rank), but admissions officers also want to know a little about you as a person. One of the ways they do this is by asking for letters of recommendation—typically from a couple of teachers and the college guidance counselor (but sometimes also from a person outside your school). These letters give a third-person perspective on some of your strengths, both intellectual and personal. You get to pick the recommenders—the people who, all things considered, will put you in the best light and, hopefully, say positive and distinctive things about you. But how to pick? Which of the possibly dozens of high school teachers that you have had should you choose? (And is there any way (short of bribery) to ensure that they write a really good letter for you?) Are letters from people outside your school—clergy folk, politicians, businesspeople, pillars of your community—at all helpful? If so, when? Our ten tips are sure to help you answer all these questions.

1. Ask for recommendations from teachers in core subjects. While some colleges tell you exactly which kind of recommendation they prefer (e.g., one science or math teacher and one English teacher), the majority of schools will leave it up to you to figure out who knows your work best. Even so, in most cases you should stick to the core disciplines: English, math, history, science, and foreign language. Like it or not, many colleges consider your performance in these to be the best predictors of how you'll do at college and, hence, want to see what those teachers have to say about your abilities in those areas.

EXTRA POINTER. Some specialized majors, such as engineering, music performance, art, or drama, will ask for very specific recommendations from particular disciplines, knowing that the skills necessary for success in that academic program will be found in those types of recommendations. Read the fine print of the application instructions because these colleges will tell you exactly what recommendations they prefer.

2. Pick teachers you've had in your junior (or, in some cases, senior) year. Admissions officers want to have the most current information about you when making their decisions, so ask teachers who have had you recently. For most students this means a teacher in a year-long course in your junior year (though, if you're filing your application toward the end of your first semester of twelfth grade or after January 1 of your senior year, a twelfth-grade teacher can be an excellent choice). Not only will they have had you in their recent memory—who can really remember that student they had two years ago in ninth grade?—but also they're likely to have taught you an advanced course, which can provide a better basis for evaluating you than that intro to general science that was required of all ninth-graders.

3. Pick teachers who know you really well. The best recommendations will come from teachers on whom you've made a strong and good impression and who can write knowledgeable, specific information about your intellectual abilities and personal gifts. A teacher who barely knows your name, but gave you an A in his or her course—even in an AP or honors course—is sometimes not as good a choice as a teacher you worked with closely but only gave you a B+. (Of course, if you have a teacher who knows you really well and who gave you an A—well, that's a match made in heaven.)

REALITY CHECK. Everything else being equal, if you have a choice between a teacher who gave you an A and a teacher who gave you a B, pick the A giver. Think about it. The teacher who gave you a B probably didn't think you were one of the best students in that very class (while the A giver probably thought of you very favorably in relation to your classmates in that class).

4. Stack the deck. Many teachers work with hundreds of students over the course of any given year, so the finer details of many of their students are lost in the shuffle (or perhaps were never there). When you ask your recommender for the letter of recommendation, be sure to offer some details to hang his or her memory on: for example, projects you enjoyed, concepts you remember, or even your reasons for picking this teacher (in the last case don't lay it on too thick). Highlighting a few points about your candidacy can often make for a much better letter—and make it much easier for your teacher to write it.

 5-STAR TIP. Ask your teacher if there are any additional materials that he or she would find useful in composing the letter. Some teachers might like to see a copy of your application or personal statement, a previous paper or problem set you did in their class, a project description, or just a bulleted tear (or brag) sheet of what you're up to these days. This is your chance to insinuate certain points into the letter.

 EPIC FAIL! No matter the process for getting recommendations in your high school, your parents shouldn't be involved. Teachers hate that; after all, it's your responsibility and your application, not your parents'. The only thing worse? Trying to tell a teacher what to put in a recommendation ("Be sure to mention how hard a worker I am … "). That'll really get their ire up.

5. Attend to any hesitation. Sometimes your memory of a stellar performance in a particular class isn't quite the same as your teacher's. When this happens, the teacher might be reluctant to write for you or might write a tepid or less than fully enthusiastic letter. Whenever you ask for a letter of recommendation, be on the lookout for any signs of hesitation on the part of the potential recommender— words such as, "I'm not sure I'm the best choice to be writing for you" or "what other teachers have you considered?" If you're not sure whether the teacher is expressing misgivings, you might simply ask him or her, "Do you know my work well enough to write me a good recommendation?" Then listen, very, very carefully, to the answer—and if there's any nontrivial hesitation expressed, find another recommender.

6. Use the college or guidance counselor. In addition to writing his or her own, overarching, letter (for which tip 4 applies), the college counselor can in many cases help you pick your other recommenders. Though he or she won't typically tell you who writes the best letters—after all, what college counselor wants to go on record dissing some teacher?—he or she can give you helpful advice about which teachers will be able to write most knowledgeably about you, and which teachers' recommendations will amplify points made elsewhere in your application. Sometimes a third-party perspective—from someone who knows both you and your teachers—can be very useful.

7. Avoid outside letters (except when they really add something). Admissions officers leave the door open for extra recommendation letters from outside people in your life, but in most cases they really don't want them; in fact, there's an old admission officers' saw: "The thicker the application file, the thicker the student." Take special care when considering whether to include outside letters of support. If some letter truly provides an insight that you would consider special or unique, then it's good. But general letters from your scoutmaster, clergy person, family friend, or (gasp) local politician—which boil down to "he's a nice kid, I like him ... " or "I spent a weekend with her, and she was really polite and respectful"—are best left out.

 BEST-KEPT SECRET. Of course, if the outside letter comes from someone who is a real expert in your proposed major or field of study—say, from a summer internship, experience in a lab, service project, college course, or relevant work experience—then by all means go for it. Sometimes an outside expert can comment more knowledgeably—and convincingly—than a high school teacher you had in some general area of study, and can really make your application stand out from the rest—especially if the person really knows you and really has something complimentary to say.

8. Be super-polite. No matter whom you ask to write, bring out the depths of your mature, respectful, and polite self. Thoughtful recommendations take time to write, and should be seen as a favor to you, not something to be expected. So a well-mannered question such as, "Ms. S., I'm planning to apply to college this fall and was wondering if you might be willing to write a letter of recommendation on my behalf," will go over much better than, "Yo, Mr. T., I need someone to write a rec for me. How 'bout you?" Teachers have considerable discretion in what they write; there's no rule book of what teachers have to say in their letters. So how you present yourself when asking for the letter can have an effect on how the recommender thinks of you when writing the letter—which, in turn, can affect how exactly he or she shades your letter.

EXTRA POINTER. Be sure to tell your teacher how much you appreciate his or her writing for you, once they have agreed, and thank them profusely when you get into those colleges they've recommended you to. People notice these small niceties and, who knows, you might need a letter from them later, perhaps for a fellowship, internship, or other purpose.

---

9. Attend to the timing. Some teachers like to get requests for letters before the summer break and others are happy to get requests in the fall, sometimes up to a couple of weeks before the deadline. Find out what your possible recommender would like. And, as the deadline draws near, it wouldn't be a half-bad idea to e-mail him or her (politely and respectfully, of course) to see that your recommender has actually submitted the letter.

10. Sign the waiver. The Common App asks you to sign a waiver to your right to read the letters of recommendation. Do so. A letter writer who knows that you're not going be reading his or her letter can write more candid—and, in some cases, stronger—comments about you and your work. Once in a while he or she can even write comparative judgments about how you stand relative to other students in the school—that he or she would never write if he or she knew you were going to be seeing them. And, if in one way or other, you ever come across a letter (say, you get a hard copy of the letter to mail to the college), don't take a glance. That's a breach of confidentiality—and, in any case, you don't want to know what your letters say.

8 Secrets for Answering the Supplemental Questions

Thought you were out of the water? You've finished the dreaded personal essay and got your lists of activities neatly laid out. But wait, for many colleges there are the supplemental questions—sometimes shorter and sometimes longer questions that colleges ask to find out a little more about you as a person and how you think about things (including their college). Want the scoop about what colleges are looking for in these additional questions—and what answers will increase your chances of getting in? Read on.

1. Take it seriously. Put as much time into the supplements as you do to your main college essay—if not more. While in some cases the questions might seem throwaways, in truth the questions are college specific and the colleges can craft exactly the questions they want to see answered. Each college has made the choice of what's most important for them to see in you, and how you answer their questions might make the difference in whether they accept you or not in the end.

BEST-KEPT SECRET. Many times admissions officers pay more attention to the supplemental questions than to the Common App essay. Why? Because they assume the main essay has been edited, proofread, revised, reviewed by teachers, parents, and sometimes even coaches. Supplemental questions, on the other hand, are oftentimes more off-the-cuff and reactive, thus providing a better representation of the student's own thoughts and perspective.

2. Tailor your essay to each school you're applying to. The essay on the Common App is a one-size-fits-all piece of writing. But the supplemental questions can be quite specific to each school you are applying, asking not only for a little more detail on who you are (what books do you like, what your greatest accomplishment was, what one thing you'd like them to know about you) but also for more information on why you're applying to their school and how you would fit in there were you accepted (what programs attracted you, how your activities dovetail with their values, or even how your character lines up with their school mission). And, if that weren't enough, a few colleges ask you questions so bizarre that you wonder what could even constitute an answer to such a question (more on these later). Obviously, no single essay is going to be usable for all schools. Take the time to think out a good answer for each of the questions at each of the colleges (do them one at a time) and customize each application to the college it's going to.

EXTRA POINTER. Especially for questions that explicitly ask you something about the interface or fit between you and the college, take the time to probe their website (especially the admissions page and the mission of the college page) to tease out hints of what they might be looking for. Often finding a very specific feature about the college in question—and adapting or particularizing it to your exact case—can make your application stand out (for instance, block learning, service to the community, global study, open curriculum—as they apply to you).

RULE OF THUMB. If your essay reads like you could easily substitute one college name for another, you've missed the mark. College supplements are not Mad Libs where you simply write in _____ [college name] or _____[major] in the space provided.

3. Mirror their values. Sometimes you'll find that a college is asking you about your personal value structure and what you might do with it at their college. For example, one college lays out five pillars of their college (social responsibility, intercultural understanding, interdisciplinary learning, student engagement, and environmental sustainability), then asks "Incorporating one or more of our core values, how would you contribute to solving a local or global issue of importance to you?" Another college states, "Emblazoned on our University Seal is a flaming heart which symbolizes St. Augustine's passionate search to know God and love others," then goes on to ask, "What sets your heart on fire?" In answering this sort of value-laden question it's important to incorporate their values into your answer and, just as important, to show how what you do or who you are lines expresses these values.

REALITY CHECK. If you don't believe in at least one of the school's five pillars or you don't have a passionate heart about anything, you're probably not going to come up with a good essay. And if the values expressed leave you completely cold, then maybe this college isn't a good fit for you. Pass it by and try another.

4. Choose carefully. Some of the shorter answer questions might ask you to select from among the following sorts of questions: *What is your favorite book, or movie, or website? If you could invite one person to dinner, living or dead, who would it be? What intellectual experience has meant the most to you?"* Here you should give very careful thought to which individual question you pick and which individual item you choose to talk about. What you pick can often reveal as much about you as what you say.

5-STAR TIP. It's often good to pick either something more unusual—something that the person ahead of you in the stack would not have picked—or something about which you have something unusual to say. For example, think twice about picking *To Kill a Mockingbird* as you favorite book; *The Perks of Being a Wallflower* as your favorite film; or WWW.KIMKARDASHIAN .COM as your favorite website.

EPIC FAIL! Be careful about choosing controversial religious or social material as your subject matter. At many colleges, a broad variety of individuals might be reading your application, with different religious, political, and social leanings—and you wouldn't want to offend someone who might be the ultimate decider. (On the other hand, if you can demonstrate sensitivity, tolerance, or open-mindedness to some hot-button issue—well, who wouldn't like that in a future student?)

 EXTRA POINTER. When making your selection(s) of what to talk about, keep in mind that the admissions officer is performing a thought experiment: what would you be like as a college student next year. Avoid subjects that are too teen-age-ish, high-school-ish, trite, clichéd, immature, sophomoric, or just plain stupid.

 REALITY CHECK. This isn't the time for humor. *You:* "Favorite book, *Captain Underpants.*" *Admissions Officer (to him- or herself):* What courses will he or she take at our college, *Boxers 102? Thongs 407?*

   5. Show yourself. Especially when you're given a question that tries to get into your psyche, don't hold back. Challenges, failures, growth experiences, most embarrassing moments, biggest triumphs can all be occasions for incredible self-reflection and revelation to your reader of who you think you are and how you got to be who you are. Keep in mind that you're probably never going to meet this admissions officer, so you needn't be shy, reserved, or tentative. In some cases, this is your best chance to showcase who you are and to provide the admissions officer with something distinctive to remember, come choice time.

REALITY CHECK. If it turns out that your proposed answer to one of the supplemental questions veers into what you've already said in the Common App personal essay (for instance, both start talking about the same single greatest failure), find something else to write about. No one wants to read regurgitated stuff that they just read.

6. Don't sweat the simple questions. Many of the supplemental questions turn out to be surprisingly similar from one college to another. "What do you want to major in? How have you heard about their college? What work experience have you had, if any? What do you expect out of college?"—all of these are just straightforward requests to learn a little bit more about you. No trick or secrets agendas here. And, given that you don't have infinite amounts of time to do these college apps, you ought to be able to write out an answer to each of these kinds of question, then copy, repurpose, or cannibalize it each time it's asked.

EXTRA POINTER. Sometimes colleges will ask you what other schools you're applying to. You needn't show your whole hand. Rather, tell each college only schools that are similar to them and include a few that are slightly better in rank. One of the things colleges are trying to gauge is whether they have a chance to get you (and whether you'd be good to get). Put in too many schools way out of their league and they might figure they don't have a chance; too many bad schools and they could think you're not worth their while.

5-STAR TIP. On the Common App, list your collections of schools alphabetically. Each college will still be able to guess where it figures in your list, but they won't be able to figure out if you'd favor a roughly similar college over them.

7. Be clever when cleverness counts. Once in a while you encounter a question that's so bizarre or off-the-wall that you think you're applying to the University of Mars. For example, "What's so odd about odd numbers?" "If you could be raised by robots, dinosaurs, or aliens, which would you choose?" "To tweet or not to tweet?" "Are we alone?" "What's your favorite word and why?" (These are all real questions and are quoted in their entirety.) When confronted with this kind of question, you need a hook: something that in some way answers the question but also provides you a platform to build on, extend, or develop the question in an interesting and clever way (after all, if the college wasn't looking for creativity, cleverness, originality, or uniqueness, why would they be asking such a question?). Try out many alternatives before committing yourself to a single answer, test out your idea with many, many people (smart and clever people), and neither take the question too literally nor view it as an occasion for flights of fancy.

5-STAR TIP. If one of the supplemental questions asks you about something other than yourself, don't make it about yourself; make it about what they're asking. "What's so odd about odd numbers" is about odd numbers, not about you as an odd number.

ON THE WEB. You and your friends will have a great time out-clevering one another with these lists of actual college questions: WWW.ACEONLINESCHOOLS.COM/20-STRANGE-COLLEGE-APPLICATION-ESSAY-QUESTIONS and WWW.FASTWEB.COM/COLLEGE-SEARCH/ARTICLES/4156-15-CRAZY-COLLEGE-APPLICATION-ESSAY-QUESTIONS. (If you can't get enough of this sort of stuff, a Google search for "unusual college application questions" will dig up even more lists.)

8. Send in extra stuff only when required—or when you have something really good. Certain schools and/or programs—for example, art, music, theater, architecture, and others—might require you to send in supplemental materials. Check the application instructions and be sure to send them exactly what's asked (not more, not less). But if supplemental materials are optional, send something in only if it's really good. The poem you wrote when you broke up with your boy- or girlfriend and the poem that wins a prize from the American Library of Poetry are very different animals.

EXTRA POINTER. And consider sending in only a sample (the abstract, not the whole paper; a representative article from the school paper, not every issue). This is especially true as colleges increasingly scan submitted materials electronically: writings, pictures, or sketches sent in in hard copy, which are too long or too many to scan, might meet their end in the circular file. And be careful even about electronic submissions: few admissions officers will want to watch an hour-long record of your work.

BONUS TIP. If you send in a collaborative project, say a paper you coauthored with many others, identify what portion of the project is your work. Admissions officers, especially faculty members who at a few schools might evaluate your submission, are very concerned to know what exact contribution you made (very important if yours is a major contribution).

6 MAKING THE CHOICE

At this point, we hope you are sitting around with multiple acceptances—and not too many rejections. If so, you are now faced with a new and much more welcome problem: how to choose where to go in the end. Maybe you're paralyzed by the choices and have no idea how to make such a major life decision. Or maybe you don't have a minute's doubt about where you want to go. Or maybe you need to choose among a number of seemingly equally attractive options. Whatever the case, it's worth it to take a few deep breaths and think through this last stage in the college-application process in an organized fashion. Especially if you, like many folks, need to balance out your priorities for your college choice with the realities of the finances.

Congratulations on reaching a successful conclusion to your college search. You'll be sure to make the right pick if you read our

▶ Top 10 strategies for making your final choice

▶ Top 10 tips for assessing the financial aid offer

Top 10 Strategies for Making Your Final Choice

So maybe it's the classic thick envelope. Or the mailer with the words on the front, "You're In!" Or, if you're really lucky (and the school bizarre enough), the admissions staff showing up at your door with the school mascot in tow. Or perhaps it's just that you checked the website or got the e-mail, with "Congratulations" or "Welcome!" in the subject line. Whatever the case, it's your dream come true: you've gotten into college and, with any luck, a slew of colleges. It's the moment of truth: now you have to make the choice. Here's how:

1. Narrow it down. If you're lucky enough to have been accepted to a handful of colleges (or more), now's the time to pare down the field to a manageable number—two or at most three. It's impossible to make an informed and serious comparison of more than that: just like when comparing headphones, you can't keep in mind the sound quality of more than two or three, so too, in comparing colleges you won't be able to evaluate more than two or three in any real way. The first step is to eliminate any choices that fall out by themselves: safe schools are no longer needed if you've gotten into better; schools that are not strong in what you want to study can be tossed; and, most important, schools that somehow "don't feel right" are probably best dumped from consideration.

2. Decide what really matters to you in a college. At this point in the decision process, you should focus on isolating those factors that are most important to you in a college. Are you academically focused, in which case you'll be concerned about things such as student-to-faculty ratio, class size, the strength of a department or course of study, and the quality of the other students? Or is it more important to you to go to a school with a certain type of social atmosphere, sports program, or campus life? It's fine to think out the various pros and cons of each choice, but usually you won't be able to come to a decision without having some idea of which "pro" is more important to you than another and which of the "cons" is less important.

EXTRA POINTER. Don't poll everyone you know. Some students think they'll get a better idea of what they themselves want—or should want—by asking people they trust, for example, a close friend, the college counselor, or their parents. But, really, this is a time to turn inward and, difficult as it might be, figure out your own goals, desires, and priorities. For yourself.

3. Consider a revisit. Sure, you might already have visited some, or all, of the colleges still in contention. But now you have a much fuller sense of what you're looking for—and what the remaining options are. So, if you can afford it, fly or drive back to your two or three leading choices and carefully think out what it might actually be like to go to those schools.

5-STAR TIP. If on your previous trip you didn't have a chance to visit a class, stay in a dorm, or talk to a professor or an undergraduate advisor in your field of possible interest, see if you can arrange any or all of these. The admissions office might be especially disposed to facilitate these things for you, now that they know their college is in your final consideration.

5-STAR TIP. In an attempt to win you over, some schools offer special "revisit programs" or "admitted students days." Check out your choice(s) to see what's offered. But, as you participate, keep in mind that the schools are now (more than ever) trying to win you over. So don't be too impressed by the "dog days," or "probabilitas week," or "lion program" (or whatever it's called at the schools you've been admitted to).

4. Talk to someone who's there—or has recently been there. One of the best—and least considered—ways of finding out what it would be like to attend one of the colleges you're considering is to talk to someone who is currently enrolled at that school or who has recently graduated from there. Often, anecdotal evidence about how good the classes are, how friendly the people are, how good the social life is, what the college community is like, and most generally, what the experience of that college is, can be more helpful than data put out by the colleges or displayed on their website. If you don't know anyone, ask your high school counselor (or friends or family members) for names of recent graduates who might be at the schools you're considering. Even if you don't personally know students who graduated your high school ahead of you, you'll find that people are flattered when you ask them about their college experiences and will be overjoyed to hear from you.

REALITY CHECK. If possible, try to reach out to more than one student. Advice is a matter of perspective and you could get a distorted picture if you talk to only one person.

EPIC FAIL! It can be a big mistake to rely too heavily on your parent's recollection of the college in question if he or she went to that college and is a lot older than you. What mom remembers from college twenty-nine years ago when the school had 12,000 students might be very different from what the college is like now that it has 26,000 students and is a mega university.

5. Get your questions answered. Now that you've been working on getting into a college for the better part of two years, you know much more about colleges and what they have to offer (and what you're looking for). And yet, there might still be remaining questions of fact—Does the school offer this or that major? Could I put together this or that program? What is needed to get on some sports team? Do they have religious activities of the kind I want?—and also questions of opinion—Are the students competitive? Is it easy to meet people? What's the food like? What do students like to do on weekends?

At this point, it's important to take an inventory of those questions that haven't fully been answered—and that matter to *you* (after all, you're the one who's going to be attending one of these schools—not your parents, your coach, your high school counselor, or your older sibling). Then make significant efforts to get those questions answered. Figure out who at the college is equipped to address your question(s) head-on; call or e-mail them with specific questions, as many as you have to ask; and if the first person you answer blows you off or doesn't answer (as can happen, especially at a larger university), find someone else (and someone else, and someone else) to ask.

6. Disregard minor differences in prestige, visibility, or rankings. When you started your search you were trying to find colleges commensurate with your interests and abilities—and when you were mapping schools into safe, reasonable shots, and reaches. Then, the image of the college and its place in the rankings loomed large. But now—when you actually know more about what the college is about (and when, if you're like many students, you've gotten into colleges of more-or-less equal rank)—the rankings should play much less of a role in your decision. Keep in mind that minor differences, say, of five or ten places, make almost no difference in any case.

7. Pick a single-focus college—or a college on the basis of a single focus—only if you're 100 percent sure that you want that focus to be the center of your college program. In some cases, depending on how you constructed your application list, you might find yourself admitted both to single-focus schools (for instance, an engineering school, architecture school, or music conservatory) and to a series of more general colleges (for example, four-year liberal arts colleges or large state universities). Or, you might find yourself admitted to a couple of colleges that you specially picked because they were strong in some field or program, for instance, exoplanets, nanotechnology, or international relations, and to a set of liberal arts colleges that are pretty good in lots of fields.

Before you throw your lot in with a specialty college—or some college on the basis of one of its specialties—make sure you really want to commit, whole hog, to that area of study. You might not have thought of this exactly, but the more specialized the school or field, the more limited (and for some students, confining) set of courses you'll have to take; the more the students you meet will be focused on that field; and the fewer opportunities you'll have to study other areas not in the program. Sure, we realize that figuring this out requires you to guess what your future self will want to do for the next four, five, or six years; and, sure, we don't want to discourage anyone from pursuing, seriously, the field of his or her dreams; it's just that single-focus means big commitment, which shouldn't be undertaken without a big commitment.

8. Don't decide on the basis of a "scorecard." One of the most common—and in our opinion least good—ways of making your final decision is to set up a list of five or six categories, assign a percentage to each of the categories, and then calculate out the scores for each of the colleges you're considering. And the proof of this is that we've seen many students set up such metrics, figure out the scores, then adjust the original weightings to get a result they're more comfortable with—that is, that expresses their true desires. A better idea, in our experience, is to pick two of the colleges under consideration, flip a coin, tell yourself which college came up and see your gut reaction: Are you overjoyed that it came up? Or do you feel some disappointment that it wasn't the other? (Then repeat for the other pairs.) Seeing and assessing your immediate response can provide a window into where you'd really like to go.

9. Approach the wait-list with great caution. Sometimes, when students hear they've gotten on the wait-list for a college (especially when it's one of their dream schools), they're overjoyed and think "I'm in the semi-finals, I'm almost in." But before turning down an offer (or series of offers), especially if accompanied by money, for what appears to be another chance at your choice college, carefully assess whether there's anything really being offered. Ask the college's admissions office to see how many people are on the current wait-list and what your position is on it (some colleges will disclose this). And ask how many were on the wait-list last year and how many in the end got in (this, every college should be willing to tell you). At some colleges, 30 percent or more get in, and if yours is one of those, you might have reason to be optimistic. But you might be amazed to hear that at some highly desirable schools fewer than 10 percent (and in a few cases almost no one) got in from the wait-list. So you shouldn't get your hopes up there.

EXTRA POINTER. If you do decide to wait out the wait-list, be sure to put a deposit down on your second-choice school. If you get in to your school of choice, in some cases, you'll just lose your deposit at the second-choice school.

EPIC FAIL! A number of colleges reserve the right to charge you a whole semester's worth of tuition if you welch on your agreement to attend (as evidenced by your deposit and the accompanying legal agreement). So before you turn down a sure bet for a pig in the poke, make sure the sure bet won't charge you a king's ransom if you decide to go elsewhere.

BEST-KEPT SECRET. It can be a good idea to contact the admissions office of a wait-listed school and provide special arguments why you're so eager to go to their school. Also, it's sometimes possible, even at this late date, to submit additional material to bolster your case, especially if something good has arisen since you applied way back in the fall. However, different schools have different procedures: some places rank students on the wait-list (so a letter serves no function); some want one point of contact (in which case you should try your luck); and still others welcome multiple contacts (in which case you should go all out). Find out what's wanted from your college of choice.

ON THE WEB. If you'd like data on how many people got in off the wait-list at the particular college(s) you're wait-listed at, go to HTTPS://BIGFUTURE.COLLEGEBOARD.ORG/, enter the name of the college in the search box, click on the entry for that college, then click on the APPLYING tab. Last year's statistics will appear under the heading "Wait List Statistics."

 ON THE WEB. Two interesting articles about how to deal with wait-lists are

WWW.WASHINGTONPOST.COM/LOCAL/EDUCATION/STUCK-ON-A-COLLEGE-WAIT-LIST-HERES-WHAT-YOU-SHOULD-DO/2014/04/20/50F2A9B2-C650-11E3-9F37-7CE307C56815_STORY.HTML and

HTTP://COLLEGEAPPS.ABOUT.COM/OD/THEARTOFGETTINGACCEPTED/F/WAITLIST_FAQ.HTM.

10. Keep it in perspective. In the end, most people's final decision comes down to a choice between two or three colleges—and they are happy at whichever one they choose. So, don't obsess. Make a decision, all things considered, and be happy with it. And for the schools you didn't get into (if any), keep in mind that yours is not a *personal* rejection. Colleges have many criteria on which they choose their admits, and sometimes, through no fault of your own, you just don't fit the bill.

 BONUS TIP. If you've visiting one of more of the "finalists," think of how you felt as you left that college. Often the feeling you had when leaving is a good gauge of how much—or little—you really liked the college.

Top 10 Tips for Assessing the Financial Aid Offer

For some students it boils down to the money: minor differences between the colleges to which they've been accepted are eclipsed by major differences in the costs of actually going there. If you're one of these students don't be ashamed. College is a ginormous purchase and, moreover, you have to buy it each year. Most important is to figure out what it's really going to cost and which of the available options makes most sense financially—as well as academically. To help you with this last stage in the college-selection process, here are our 10 best tips for figuring out the finances.

1. Figure out *your* budget. Most of the financial aid letters you receive from a college will contain an estimated or standard budget for your first year at college. Typically, you might see the cost of tuition and fees, rooms and meals, books and supplies, transportation, and personal expenses or miscellaneous costs. But these figures are just the college's best guess about how much you will spend. You might know better. Consider how often you plan to go out and eat (and how much it costs); how often you're going to fly or drive home (and how far away you are from your parents); and how much cash you go through a week (i.e., what's to be included under "miscellaneous" expenses). Once you set your own budget estimate, you'll know if the "standard" budget is too generous, not generous enough, or just about right.

 EXTRA POINTER. Beware of items left off the estimated budget. One school says their offer is "all-inclusive *except for* health insurance, textbooks, lab fees, parking permit, laundry, and miscellaneous spending money"—which could easily run to three, four, or even five thousand dollars a year.

ON THE WEB. It can be useful to compare the cost of living in the college city or town to that of your home town. Use this tool: WWW.BANKRATE.COM/CALCULATORS/SAVINGS/MOVING-COST-OF-LIVING-CALCULATOR.ASPX.

2. Realize that loans are yours to repay—not a gift from the college. Many times—especially if the college making the offer doesn't commit to providing 100 percent of demonstrated family need *as gift*—the financial aid package will include loans, often federal loans. They could be Stafford or Perkins—or could be PLUS loans for your parents—but in every case there'll come a day where you or someone else will have to pay back the money—with interest. The average college graduate today owes almost $30,000 (about the price of a car) and will be paying it off for the next ten years (about twice the repayment period of a car). So, before taking on loans, think about how you'd feel about paying, say, $300 a month from 2020 through 2030.

 RULE OF THUMB. When borrowing money, take out federal loans first, then state loans, then private loans from banks. Not only are the rates likely to be better, the repayment terms can be longer, deferments and forbearances are possible if you find yourself in bad financial straits or go on to graduate or professional school, and in some cases the government pays the interest while you are enrolled in school.

 REALITY CHECK. Whenever taking a loan make sure you fully understand:

- ✔ the annual percentage rate (APR)

- ✔ whether the APR is fixed (stays the same throughout the repayment period) or variable (could go up when interest rates go up)

✔ the terms of repayment (how long you have to pay it off)

✔ the monthly payment (for different lengths of repayment)

✔ whether the loan is subsidized (that is, someone other than you pays the interest while you are in college and, in some cases, graduate or professional school)

✔ whether there is any origination fee (that is, additional charge that has to be paid up-front)

✔ whether the loan is for one year or the entire time you're in college

✔ whether there's the possibility of deferment or forbearance (if things go wrong health- or employment-wise)

✔ whether there are any conditions on the loan (do you have to maintain a certain GPA or take a certain number of credit hours to continue to qualify?)

✔ whether the loan is not dischargeable in a bankruptcy (that is, even if you file for bankruptcy you still owe the loan—almost always true of federal student loans)

If you have any questions—which, no doubt, you will—ask the financial aid office or the lender for clarification. And keep all documents; you might need them later.

 ON THE WEB. Use the New York State's Federal Loan Repayment Estimator, WWW.HESC.NY.GOV/PAY-FOR-COLLEGE/APPLY-FOR-FINANCIAL-AID/COMPARING-COLLEGE-AWARD-LETTERS.HTML, to determine how much the monthly payment will be on your proposed federal student loan.

Have a look at Bank of America's "Better Ways to Save," especially the section on how debt works at WWW.BETTERMONEYHABITS.COM/DEBT/HTML.

Also quite useful is WWW.KHANACADEMY.ORG/COLLEGE-ADMISSIONS/PAYING-FOR-COLLEGE, which breaks down the basics of how student loans operate.

IOHO. We don't think loans should even be called "financial *aid*." After all, the government, college, or bank is "aiding" you with your own future money (plus interest).

3. Assess your—and your parents'—level of comfort. If some of your financial aid offers include loans and some do not (or some include smaller loans) you need to gauge for yourself how much debt (multiplied by the number of years you plan to spend in college) you're able to comfortably take on. Some of this assessment, of course, depends on the assets and willingness to pay of whoever is going ultimately to pay off the loan. And some of it depends on whether you have a career track in mind and how much that career is ultimately going to pay in the first years. But keep in mind that availability of work can change; and, of course, if you bail from the career you thought you might take up, your earning power might go down or up, depending on your new choices.

EXTRA POINTER. Make sure all the signers on the loan are on board. If your parents cosign a loan or if they take out their own PLUS or private loan, they're on the hook for the whole amount if, for whatever reason, you're unable to pay. It would behoove you to discuss this with them.

BEST-KEPT SECRET. For certain service professions the government will delay the repayment period for a number of years after graduation. So if you think the military, National Guard, the Peace Corps, law enforcement, or corrections might be in your future, check out which loans offer additional, interest-free time to delay repaying your loans.

4. Keep in mind that work study is *work*. Many financial aid offers list "work study" or "college work study" as a line entry in the award. And many colleges include "expected student contribution" (which can be sizeable, sometimes four or five thousand a year) in their list of what the family needs to pay. Keep in mind that work study is, in more cases than not, *work* (not too much study). While in the good case you could be collaborating with your chemistry professor by correlating the data that he or she will use in the jointly authored articles with you, in other cases you could be the guard at the university museum or library or could work in one of the departmental offices filing reports or even working in the food service washing pots. And, if you're being expected to contribute money as student contribution, think about how many hours you'd have to work over the summer or term time to round up those four to five thousand dollars.

EXTRA POINTER. To find out how many hours a week you're signing on to do, ask how much jobs pay at the college you're considering. A simple e-mail to the financial aid office should give you the range of typical (or at least minimum) salaries.

5. Mind the gap. Some schools might not provide the entire amount you need—even by their estimates (the "estimated family contribution"). Keep in mind that if such a shortfall or gap exists, you'll have to put in more of your own resources above and beyond any loans or work study you're taking on. Not so great.

6. You needn't take it all. No matter how much the aid is presented as a "package," you needn't take it all. If, for example, some loan is not to your liking or if instead of taking work study your parents would be willing to absorb that extra cost so that you can study full time—it's perfectly acceptable to accept some lines and decline others (indeed, some colleges provide check boxes for just this purpose). Think out each component as an independent offer and choose what makes best sense for you.

7. Use the tools. There are a number of very useful tools for comparing offers from different colleges. The very basic, most user friendly include these:

College Board: HTTPS://BIGFUTURE.COLLEGEBOARD.ORG/PAY-FOR-COLLEGE/ FINANCIAL-AID-AWARDS/COMPARE-AID-CALCULATOR#

Finaid: WWW.FINAID.ORG/CALCULATORS/AWARDLETTER.PHTML and its more advanced sibling WWW.FINAID.ORG/CALCULATORS/AWARDLETTERADVANCED .PHTML

ECMC: HTTPS://COLLEGEABACUS.ORG/

the federal government's Consumer Financial Protection Bureau: WWW.CONSUMERFINANCE.GOV/PAYING-FOR-COLLEGE/COMPARE-FINANCIAL-AID- AND-COLLEGE-COST/

All very useful.

8. Balance off college and graduate school. Some students, who have only a finite amount of savings and only the willingness to take on a finite amount of debt, reason "I'll go to the cheapest college I got into and save my money for graduate or professional school." Others think, "I'll spend the money to go to the most prestigious college I can, and then, I hope, get a fellowship to pay for graduate school, medical school, law school, business school, or whatever."

What you need to know is that in different fields, different choices make the most sense. If you'll never get into a good graduate school if you didn't go to a good college, it might be prudent to focus your financial resources on college. If, however, what counts most in getting into a law or med school is your LSATs or MCATs, not what college you went to, you might want to save your money for those post college programs.

5-STAR TIP. If you, already planning to go to a graduate or professional school, inquire of a couple of such schools— particular departments, in the case of graduate schools—how they do admissions. Often they'll be able to give you good advice about when to spend savings, when to take on debt, and how realistic it is to expect a fellowship for graduate or professional schools.

9. Consider an appeal. Sometimes it turns out that you think the award is vastly lower than what you need to go to that school. Call up or e-mail the financial aid office and explain—objectively—why you think you need more aid. If there's been some change in your family situation since you applied (say, a parent has lost his or her job or there have been unexpected medical expenses), or if you think the college has somehow misfigured the award, or if the college has some very special program that you would enroll in if only you could afford to go to that college—by all means call any of these things to the financial aid office's attention. Be prepared to document whatever you are claiming.

REALITY CHECK. It usually doesn't help your case to argue that "my parent doesn't think your estimate of what he or she should pay is right." Colleges have their own way of determining how much they can expect from a parent and although, in some cases, the parent might think he or she should be paying only half of what the college wants, the college will usually stick to its own determination if you argue in this way.

ON THE WEB. An interesting and probing article on the issue of appeals can be found at WWW.NYTIMES.COM/2014/04/05/YOUR-MONEY/PAYING-FOR-COLLEGE/FOR-MANY-FAMILIES-COLLEGE-FINANCIAL-AID-PACKAGES-ARE-WORTH-AN-APPEAL.HTML?_R=0.

10. Shop it around. In spite of the fact that the "official financial aid offer" looks very official, it's not always set in stone. If you have received a better offer from a relevant alternative to the school in question, by all means contact them. Be prepared to e-mail or fax them the other offer and keep in mind that colleges have their own ideas about what schools they ought to be competing against (and how much resources they have to commit to winning away students from other schools). And emphasize that—and why—you'd really like to go to the college you're petitioning and what you'd bring to that college's community.

BEST-KEPT SECRET. Not too many people know this but some colleges maintain lists of, or policies about, which other college offers they'll match (though they probably won't show you the lists or tell you the policies). So, in certain cases, you have a good shot.

BY THE SAME AUTHORS. If you've enjoyed this book and have gotten in to the college of your choice, you might enjoy reading *The Secrets of College Success: Over 800 Tips, Techniques, and Strategies Revealed* (Second Edition) by Professors Lynn F. Jacobs and Jeremy S. Hyman. Why not build success on success? Available wherever books are sold.

APPENDIX

HOW ADMISSIONS DECISIONS ARE MADE

Ted Spencer
Associate Vice Provost and Executive Director, Office of
Undergraduate Admissions, University of Michigan

(from a presentation given at the 2014 Harvard Summer
Institute on College Admissions)

Introduction

When preparing the presentation, "How Admissions Decisions Are Made," the main purpose was to explain the process that takes place in most selective universities in the country.

I know that for the public, and even often for members of the admissions profession, both at the K-12 level as well as in higher ed, the decisions that many colleges make may appear to be confusing and arbitrary. Like most organizations or businesses, the reasons why we do what we do are based on set goals that will best allow us to accomplish our mission. Within the higher education community, it is based on the mission statements or guidelines established to meet the unique goals of that college or university.

After researching the guidelines of many other selective institutions, we developed a set of guidelines that would allow us to evaluate a broad range of criteria as part of the individual review of every application. It was designed primarily to be holistic, because it is not based solely on grades and test scores, but rather allowed us to look at the applicants' many achievements, thereby giving students more opportunities to tell us about themselves.

Finally, our approach to holistic review has resulted in more consistent review of a record number of applications. In addition, considering an applicant's overall academic accomplishments and extra-curricular achievements has allowed us to successfully meet our goal of admitting and retaining some of the best and brightest students from many diverse backgrounds.

Theodore L. Spencer
Senior Advisor on Admissions Outreach
The University of Michigan

During the evaluation process, readers and admissions counselors will consider a broad range of criteria as part of the individualized review of every application.

Academic Achievement, Quality, and Potential

Direct Measures

- Cumulative GPA

- Pattern of grade improvement during high school

- Quality of curriculum

  - Solid college-prep curriculum (4 years in each subject)

  - Strength of senior year courses

  - Core (required) curriculum/courses beyond core curriculum

  - AP, IB and honors / college courses while in H.S.

- Test scores (SAT I and II, ACT, AP, etc.)

- Internships in area of academic interest

- Participation in enrichment or outreach programs

- Class rank

Academic Achievement, Quality and Potential (contd.)

Educational Environment

▶ Strength of curriculum (including availability of AP, IB, honors)

▶ Average SAT I and/or ACT scores

▶ Percentage attending 4-year colleges

▶ Competitive grading system in high school

▶ Competitiveness of class

▶ Academically disadvantaged school

Evaluative Measures

▶ Academic recognition and awards

▶ Artistic talent

▶ Depth in one or more academic areas related to student interests

▶ Evidence of academic passion

▶ Grasp of world events

▶ Independent academic research

▶ Intellectual curiosity

▶ Writing quality—content, style, originality, risk taking

Characteristics and Attributes

Personal Background

- ▶ Alumni connection

- ▶ Cultural awareness/experiences

- ▶ First generation to go to college from family

- ▶ Low-economic family background

- ▶ Underrepresented minority (for reporting purposes only)

- ▶ Personal disadvantage

- ▶ Professional diversity

- ▶ Faculty/staff connection

- ▶ Military veteran/Peace Corps, America Corps, etc.

Geographic Considerations

- ▶ In-state resident

- ▶ Economically disadvantaged region

- ▶ From school with few or no previous applicants

Characteristics and Attributes (contd.)

Extracurricular Activities, Service, and Leadership

▶ Awards and honors (athletic, artistic, musical, civic)

▶ Quality and depth of involvement

▶ Leadership

▶ Community service

▶ Impact student's involvement had on school and/or community

▶ Scholarship athlete

▶ Work experience

Extenuating Circumstances

▶ Overcoming personal adversity/ unusual hardships

▶ Language spoken at home/ESL

▶ Frequent moves/many different schools

Other Considerations

▶ Demonstrated interest in college/good match

▶ Strong personal statement

Recommendations

Counselor & Teacher Recommendations

▶ Character

▶ Civic and cultural awareness/diverse perspective/tolerance

▶ Commitment

▶ Intellectual independence/enthusiasm for learning/risk taking

▶ Creativity/artistic talent

▶ Concern for others/community

▶ Motivation/determination/grit/effort/initiative/ persistence/tenacity

▶ Leadership potential/maturity/responsibility

College Essay Writing Tips

▶ Be honest—write about something small in scale; a story only you can tell in your own words.

▶ Let your voice be heard.

▶ If there is something strange about your record, you should explain it (e.g., academic trends primarily).

▶ You should write about something that's important to you.

▶ Don't try to guess about which topic we want to read.

▶ Content, style, originality—cautiously humorous, risk taking.

▶ Discuss unique talents.

▶ How would you describe the strength and weaknesses of the topic—your point of view—regarding the essay question?

▶ Interesting or unique insights about a particular topic are welcome.

▶ Something that will enlighten us about yourself as it relates to the chosen topic.

▶ Use language with which you are familiar.

▶ Don't try to borrow someone else's phrases.

▶ The essay should show your character and personality—not just bragging about your list of accomplishments.

▶ Answer the question when you choose a topic—follow the directions, length, and format.

▶ Most readers look for essays that are persuasive and somewhat argumentative.

Examining the Applicant's File: Some Reading Tips

An Admissions Committee carefully reviews information provided by the student and the high school. To help you read your files, here are a few questions on each section of the application. Please carefully read the admissions cases and take notes on the candidate rating form.

Personal Information

Is there anything about the student's background or family information that stands out in relation to the college to which they are applying? Are there any special circumstances of which you should be aware when evaluating the more objective parts of the application?

Transcript

What kind of grades had the student received over the years? Is there a trend—an upward or downward one? Has the student taken advanced and/or challenging classes? (Look at the high school profiles to get a brief sketch of what is offered. Does the high school have strict prerequisites for entrance into these courses?) If shown on the transcript, what kind of program does the student plan to take in the senior year—is it challenging or weak? What are the student's curricular interests? If available, where does the student rank? (Does the high school provide rank?)

SAT I/ACT/SAT II

What are the student's SAT or ACT scores? Are there areas that are significantly higher or lower? How strong are the SAT II scores? Do they show special proficiencies in specific subject areas? How do the scores fit the score ranges on the college profiles? (How important do you think that test scores will be in the evaluation process?) Do the SAT/ACT scores correlate with the student's GPA? Is one significantly higher than the other?

Activities

What has the student done outside the classroom, both in school and out of school? How much time has the student committed to those activities? How much depth is presented? Has the student pursued an activity over a sustained period? Has the student pursued leadership roles within those activities?

Essay

Does the essay tell you something about the student beyond the transcript? What did you learn? What qualities or talents does the student reveal? Do you hear the student's voice? Do you get a sense of the student as a person? Have they done an effective job of telling their story? Are the grammar, spelling, and punctuation correct?

Letters of Recommendation

What two or three things have you learned about the applicant through the recommendation? What struck the teacher most about the student? How positive or enthusiastic is the recommendation? Is there information that will help the admission committee determine how capable the student is of meeting the academic demands of the college?

High School/College Profiles

What can the admissions committee learn from the high school profile that might assist them? How might the colleges help us learn which student might be the best fit for their college? Does the high school profile give you information that might better help you understand the student's educational opportunities and accomplishments? (How does the school profile present its own academic program?)

Freshman Application Rating Sheet   Appendix A

Secondary School Academic Performance	Comments:	Overall:

1. Cumulative GPA
Pattern of grade improvement in high school
2. Quality of curriculum:
 	
  a. Solid college-prep curr. (4 yrs. in each subject)
  b. Strength of senior year courses
  c. Core (required) courses beyond core curriculum
  d. AP, IB, and honors/college courses while in HS
 	
3. **Test scores (ACT, SAT, TOEFL, MELAB, IELTS etc.)**
(NOTE: Pre-printed scores are "best composite" received. Review applicant profile and/or high school transcript for additional test scores).
4. **Academic interest(s)**
5. **Class Rank**
6. **Other**		

Educational Environment	**Comments:**	**Overall:**
1. Strength of curriculum (incl. availability of AP, IB, honors) 2. Average SAT and/or ACT scores 3. Percentage attending 4-year colleges 4. Competitive grading system in high school 5. Competitiveness of class 6. Academically disadvantaged school 7. Other		
Counselor and Teacher Recommendations	**Comments:**	**Overall:**
1. Character 2. Civic and cultural awareness/diverse perspective/tolerance 3. Commitment to high ideals 4. Intellectual independence/enthusiasm for learning/risk taking 5. Creativity/artistic talent 6. Concern for others/community 7. Motivation/determination/effort/initiative/persistence/tenacity 8. Leadership potential/maturity/responsibility 9. Other		

Personal Background	Comments:	Overall:

1. Cultural awareness/experiences
2. Socioeconomic and educational background
 	
   a. First generation to go to college in family
   b. Low economic family background
   c. Economically disadvantaged region
 	
3. Geographical considerations
 	
   a. In-state resident
   b. Under-represented geographic area
 	
4. Awards/honors (academic, athletic, artistic, musical, civic)
5. Extracurricular activities, service, and leadership
6. Participation in enrichment or outreach programs
7. Alumni relationships
8. Scholarship athlete
9. Work experience
10. Other (e.g. military, Peace Corp service: specify)		

Evaluative Measures	**Comments:**	**Overall:**
1. Depth in one or more academic areas of student's interests 2. Evidence of academic passion 3. Grasp of world events 4. Independent academic research 5. Intellectual curiosity 6. Artistic talent 7. Writing quality: content, style, originality, risk taking 8. Other		
Extenuating Circumstances	**Comments:**	**Overall:**
1. Overcoming personal adversity/disadvantage/unusual hardships 2. Language spoken at home/ESL 3. Frequent moves, many different schools 4. Other	Native:	
Other Considerations	**Comments:**	**Overall:**
1. Demonstrated interest in school or college/good match 2. Strong personal statement 3. Other		

(continued)

Overall Comments/Recommendations/Reservations:

EVALUATOR (circle) #1or#2: Initials _____ Date:_____/ ____/ **20**____ Data Entry: Initials/Date_____

_____

OUTSTANDING	EXCELLENT	GOOD	AVERAGE/FAIR	BELOW AVG/POOR
(Circle) HA+ HA HA -	A+A A-	AR+ AR AR-	DR+DR DR-	D+ D D-

Recommendations: CSP_____AEE_____Routing Flag: _____

EVALUATOR #3 or VALIDATOR: Initials _____ Date:_____/ ____/ **20**____   Data Entry: Initials/Date_____

_____

OUTSTANDING	EXCELLENT	GOOD	AVERAGE/FAIR	BELOW AVG/POOR
(Circle) HA+ HA HA -	A+A A-	AR+ AR AR-	DR+DR DR-	D+ D D-

Final Recommendations: CSP _____ AEE _____ Routing Flag: _____
REFER TO COMMITTEE: LSA_____ENG_____ARC

FINAL COMMITTEE: Initials _____ Date:_____/ ____/ **20**____   Data Entry: Initials/Date_____

_____

OUTSTANDING	EXCELLENT	GOOD	AVERAGE/FAIR	BELOW AVG/POOR
(Circle) HA+ HA HA -	A+A A-	AR+ AR AR-	DR+DR DR-	D+ D D-

Recommendations: CSP_____AEE_____Routing Flag: _____

Rating scale: Outstanding—Excellent—Good—Average/Fair—Below Average/Poor

For most categories, the applicant may receive one of the above evaluation ratings. In some instances, the applicant's record will be assessed on the evidence of certain characteristics and attributes and the rating scale will not be applicable (e.g. personal background, geographical considerations). For these areas, the reviewer should assess the applicant's contributions to the University in qualifying terms. The reviewer will need to provide comments that support the recommended buckets.

2009–10

WEB RESOURCES

Here is an alphabetical list of all the URLs in the book complete with the page number(s) on which each appears:

CAMPUSVISIT.COM (78)

CAPPEX.COM (78)

EDVISORS.COM (32, 33)

GOSEECAMPUS.COM (78)

HTTP://ADMISSIONS.CORNELL.EDU/APPLY/WHAT-CORNELL-LOOKS (186)

HTTP://BLOG.COMMONAPP.ORG/2015/03/31/2015-2016-ESSAY-PROMPTS/ (195)

HTTP://COLLEGEAPPS.ABOUT.COM/OD/THEARTOFGETTINGACCEPTED/F/WAITLIST_FAQ.HTM (222)

HTTP://COLLEGEINSIGHT.ORG/ (30)

HTTP://EDUCATION.TI.COM/EN/US/DOWNLOADS-AND-ACTIVITIES?ACTIVE=GUIDEBOOKS (148)

HTTP://FAIRTEST.ORG/UNIVERSITY/OPTIONAL (114)

HTTP://GRAPHING-CALCULATOR-REVIEW.TOPTENREVIEWS.COM/ (145)

HTTP://H20180.WWW2.HP.COM/APPS/LOOKUP?H_PAGETYPE=S-003&H_CLIENT=Z-A-R1002--3&H_PAGE=INDEX&H_LANG=EN&H_CC=US&JUMPID=HPR_R1002_USEN_LINK1 (148)

HTTP://NCES.ED.GOV/COLLEGENAVIGATOR (30)

HTTP://NICHE.COM/ (28)

HTTP://ONLINE.WSJ.COM/ARTICLES/HOW-TO-WINTHE-COLLEGE-SCHOLARSHIP-GAME-1408126980 (64)

HTTP://PROFESSIONALS.COLLEGEBOARD.COM/PROFDOWNLOAD/SAT-MATHEMATICSREVIEW.PDF (138)

WWW.COLLEGERESULTS.ORG (30)

WWW.COLLEGERESULTS.ORG/SEARCH_BASIC.ASPX (23)

WWW.COLLEGEXPRESS.COM/LISTS/LIST/COLLEGES-THAT-MEET-THEFINANCIAL-NEEDS-OF-STUDENTS/349/ (62)

WWW.COMPASSPREP.COM/WP-CONTENT/UPLOADS/2014/12/REDESIGNED-SAT-SPEC-SHEET.PDF (171)

WWW.CONSUMERFINANCE.GOV/PAYING-FOR-COLLEGE/COMPARE-FINANCIAL-AIDAND-COLLEGE-COST/ (228)

WWW.ECAMPUSTOURS.COM (28)

WWW.EDVISORS.COM/SCHOLARSHIPS (33)

WWW.EXAMINER.COM/ARTICLE/COLLEGES-THAT-DO-NOT-SUPERSCORETHE-SAT (118)

WWW.FAIRTEST.ORG (29)

WWW.FASTWEB.COM (32)

WWW.FASTWEB.COM/COLLEGESEARCH/ARTICLES/4156-15-CRAZY-COLLEGE-APPLICATION-ESSAYQUESTIONS (213)

WWW.FINAID.ORG/CALCULATORS/AWARDLETTER.PHTML (228)

WWW.FINAID.ORG/CALCULATORS/AWARDLETTERADVANCED.PHTML (228)

WWW.FINAID.ORG/QUESTIONS/DIVORCE.PHTML (66)

WWW.FORBES.COM/SITES/TROYONINK/2014/02/14/HOW-ASSETSHURT-COLLEGE-AID-ELIGIBILITY-ON-FAFSA-AND-CSS-PROFILE/ (60)

WWW.FORBES.COM/SITES/TROYONINK/2014/11/28/2015-GUIDE-TO-FAFSA-CSS-PROFILE-COLLEGE-FINANCIAL-AIDAND-EXPECTED-FAMILY-CONTRIBUTION-EFC/ (58)

WWW.FORBES.COM/SITES/TROYONINK/2015/02/28/PAYING-FOR-COLLEGE-HOWTO-POSITION-ASSETS-TO-QUALIFY-FOR-MORE-COLLEGE-FINANCIAL-AID/ (60)

WWW.HESC.NY.GOV/PAY-FOR-COLLEGE/APPLYFOR-FINANCIAL-AID/COMPARING-COLLEGE-AWARD-LETTERS.HTML (225)

WWW.KHANACADEMY.ORG/COLLEGEADMISSIONS/PAYING-FOR-COLLEGE (226)

WWW.KHANACADEMY.ORG/SAT (123)

WWW.KHANACADEMY.ORG/TEST-PREP/SAT/FULL-LENGTH-SAT-1 (123)

WWW.KIPLINGER.COM/TOOL/COLLEGE/T014-S001-KIPLINGER-S-BEST-VALUES-IN-PRIVATE-COLLEGES/INDEX.PHP?TABLE=ALL (62)

WWW.KNOWHOW2GO.ORG (31)

WWW.LIBRARY.UIUC.EDU/EDX/RANKINGS.HTM (29)

WWW.LINKEDIN.COM (198)

WWW.MERITAID.COM (33)

WWW.NACACNET.ORG/STUDENTINFO/PAGES/DEFAULT.ASPX (27)

WWW.NYTIMES.COM/2006/07/30/EDUCATION/EDLIFE/INNOVATION.HTML?_R=0 (54)

WWW.NYTIMES.COM/2014/04/05/YOURMONEY/PAYING-FOR-COLLEGE/FOR-MANY-FAMILIES-COLLEGE-FINANCIAL-AIDPACKAGES-ARE-WORTH-AN-APPEAL.HTML?_R=0 (230)

WWW.NYTIMES.COM/2014/11/16/NYREGION/APPLICATIONS-BY-THEDOZEN-AS-ANXIOUS-STUDENTS-HEDGE-COLLEGE-BETS.HTML?_R=1 (181)

WWW.NYTIMES.COM/INTERACTIVE/2012/07/08/EDUCATION/EDLIFE/8EDLIFE_CHART.HTML (62)

WWW.PARCHMENT.COM (30)

WWW.PETERSONS.COM (33)

WWW.PROPUBLICA.ORG/ARTICLE/THE-ADMISSION-ARMS-RACE-SIX-WAYSCOLLEGES-CAN-GAME-THEIR-NUMBERS (54)

WWW.SAT.COLLEGEBOARD.ORG/SCORES (117)

WWW.SCHOLARSHIPEXPERTS.COM (33)

WWW.SCHOLARSHIPPOINTS.COM (33)

WWW.SCHOLARSHIPS.COM (33)

WWW.SCHOLARSHIPS.COM/FINANCIAL-AID/COLLEGE-SCHOLARSHIPS/SCHOLARSHIPS-BY-STATE/ (64)

WWW.STSTRAVEL.COM/COLLEGE-SPRINGBREAK-DATES (78)

WWW.STUDENTSCHOLARSHIPSEARCH.COM (32)

WWW.THECOLLEGESOLUTION.COM/LIST-OF-COLLEGES-THAT-MEET-100-OF-FINANCIAL-NEED/ (62)

WWW.USNEWS.COM/EDUCATION (26)

WWW.USNEWS.COM/EDUCATION/BEST-COLLEGES/PAYING-FORCOLLEGE/ARTICLES/2013/09/18/COLLEGES-THAT-CLAIM-TO-MEET-FULLFINANCIAL-NEED-2014 (62)

WWW.USNEWS.COM/EDUCATION/BEST-COLLEGES/PAYING-FORCOLLEGE/ARTICLES/2014/09/15/COLLEGES-AND-UNIVERSITIES-THAT-CLAIMTO-MEET-FULL-FINANCIAL-NEED (178)

WWW.USNEWS.COM/EDUCATION/BEST-COLLEGES/THE-SHORT-LIST-COLLEGE/ARTICLES/2014/09/16/COLLEGES-THAT-CHARGETHE-MOST-FOR-APPLYINGN (181)

WWW.USNEWS.COM/USNEWS/STORE/COLLEGE_COMPASS.HTM (27)

WWW.WASHINGTONPOST.COM/LOCAL/EDUCATION/STUCK-ON-ACOLLEGE-WAIT-LIST-HERES-WHAT-YOU-SHOULD-DO/2014/04/20/50F2A9B2-C650-11E3-9F37-7CE307C56815_STORY.HTML (222)

WWW.YOUCANGO.COLLEGEBOARD.ORG (31)

INDEX